G͡

RELATIONSHIPS

not your way

Helena Webster

Published by Austin Publishing

AUSTIN PUBLISHING
P. O. Box 52
Clarkston, Georgia 30021
(404) 508-8200

Printed by: Morris Publishing
                P.O. Box 2110
                Kearney, NE 68847

Scripture quotations in this publication are from the Holy Bible: New International Version (NIV).

Manufactured in the United States of America.

ISBN 0-9670001-0-6

To order this title by mail, please include price of book plus $2.50 handling by per order, and $1.00 for each book ordered. Send to: Austin Publishing, P.O. Box 52, Clarkston, Ga 30021.

To God, my parents Mr. and Mrs. Thornton Lewis Webster, Sr. and my son Austin , I appreciate your love, support and patience

DEDICATION

My heavenly Father, I thank You with all my heart for allowing my dreams to become reality. You are truly an awesome God and I am humbled by Your love for me. You have given me a whole new purpose, Father, and I will forever praise Your holy name. I cannot imagine life without You because You are my only source of strength.

It is to You, I dedicate this book because of Your unfailing love for me. Without You, it would have no meaning–without You, it could never have been published---and without You Lord, I would not have been able to share what You have given me with others. I am grateful and will never take the things You have done for me for granted. You are my Rock and my fortress and all that I will ever need to bring me joy. In You, Father, I have found peace and a resting place.

To God be the glory.

HOW TO CONTACT THE AUTHOR

Helena Webster is available to speak at various functions nationwide upon your request. Your organization, family, friends, co-workers and significant other would greatly benefit from hearing this magnificent speaker. Inquiries about her availability for speeches and seminars should be directed to the address below. Readers are also encouraged to contact the author with comments and ideas for future editions.

Helena Webster
c/o Austin Publishing
P.O. Box 52
Clarkston, Georgia 30021
(404) 508-8200

TABLE OF CONTENTS

ACKNOWLEDGMENTS

There are so many individuals that made this book become a reality. First to my Dad, Thornton Lewis Webster Sr., you are the most loving and gentle man I have ever known. Thank you for teaching me 'everything I know.' You are the 'Wind Beneath My Wings' and I love you with all my heart and soul.

No one has a better friend than Jacqueline Scott. From the beginning, she took on the task of assisting me with a smile on her face. She had the integrity to challenge me and the sensitivity to encourage me along the way. She worked hard feeling the pressure of the deadline along with me, and I am very grateful for her efforts, continued love and support. You are indispensable Mrs. Scott!

Marvin Blow, my forever friend. I thank you for always being the 'Friend who just stands by.' My highs have been your highs and my lows your lows. You have never wavered where our friendship is concerned, and I cannot thank you enough for just being there. With a friend like you in my corner, I will never wonder if I have somewhere to turn.

To the greatest sister in the world, Lacresia Webster, I cannot thank you enough for just being *you*. I am truly blessed to have a sister like you. We have been through so much together I would not trade the memories we have shared for anything. You are truly a gift from above.

To two of the greatest professors Clark Atlanta University has ever seen, Dr. Gale Horton and Dr. Sandra Foster, I thank both of you for everything you have taught me this past year about life, people and getting the job done. Both of you have always taken the time to say an encouraging word and offer sound advice. I am grateful to you for being more than 'professors' but also taking an interest in the needs of the students you serve. I am appreciative of your efforts and I take my hat off to both of you. By the way Dr. Foster, I met my deadline.

To the Church of Christ, Atlanta, Georgia you all have taught me what *"Spirituality, Belief and Faithfulness"* are about. I appreciate your examples of children living for Christ. For everyone who took a moment to answer a question or voice an opinion, thank you for challenging me to ask myself *"Can I Relate?"* To the most ultra-feminine girl in the world, my mom, Ruthie Webster thank you for helping me *"Become a Woman."* To Steve and Kim Sapp, I appreciate the advice you provided at the retreat on *"Dating."* To my son Austin for helping me realize that I really must *"Get it Together."* My friend, my confidante and sister in Christ, Stephanie Johnson thank you for always being there and for teaching me what it means to *"Encourage and Support."* My brother Kevin Darnell Webster and his wife Machel you both have the ability to educate anyone about what it takes to be happily *"Married."* Lastly, Mark Hicks, whose patience and understanding taught me *"How to Build and Sustain a Relationship,"* you have proven to be a true friend, not to mention an awesome man of God.

I thank each of you for being there in times of need. Your encouragement, advice and assistance are deeply appreciated. I thank you all and may you continue to be Blessed always!

INTRODUCTION

This book is about you and your ability to relate. Whether single, married or somewhere in between–this book is sure to help you discover ways to improve your relationships. In these chapters you will discover new easy techniques that guarantee successful relationships with people, especially your significant other.

The challenge is to grow as you read each chapter becoming more knowledgeable about how to build healthy long-lasting relationships God's way. Use God's word to learn how to interact in a righteous manner.

Participating in relationships that please God is a guarantee that you are part of a relationship with unlimited possibilities of true happiness. Growth can only take place with a conscious effort on your part. The end result is a change in the way you approach your family, friends, co-workers, and everyone with whom you come in contact,...but most importantly your mate. Scripturally based throughout to support the facts presented, this book will inform you about how you can have a spiritual relationship. You are sure to find this as one of the most helpful tools ever written.

This book will challenge you, open your heart, and move you to live as the righteous woman that you are called to be. Expect life-changing results as you allow His words to guide you and prepare you for relationships that are fulfilling and rewarding.

After applying this knowledge, you will relate with confidence, persevere with patience and respond with love. You will become an expert on relating to others and will transform in the woman of God you desire to be.

CHAPTER 1

SPIRITUALITY, BELIEF AND FAITHFULNESS

----

*Jesus replied, "If you have faith and no
doubt, not only can you do what was done
to the fig tree, but also you can say to this
mountain, 'Go throw yourself into the sea,'
and it will be done. If you believe, you will
receive whatever you ask for in prayer."*

Matthew 21: 21-22

Spirituality is not how many times you attend church service,
how often you pray or how well you lay hands or speak in tongues.
Spirituality is the life-giving principle of a human being. It is the
soul. It is who you are with or without the physical actions,
metaphysical make-up or behavior patterns.

1

Spirituality comes from within and is what moves us to be in direct relationship with God through His word. "God is spirit, and his worshipers must worship in spirit and in truth" (John 4:24). Before you can be in a relationship with anyone else, you must be in relationship with God. To be in a relationship with God, you must know what His word says. It is important to understand the impact God's word has on your life and to be obedient to His word, applying it daily so that when you are tempted you will not give in to sin. "Watch and pray so that you will not fall into temptation. The spirit is willing, but the body is weak" (Matthew 26:41).

As a spiritual woman, you are now a different woman. Your primary focus in life is to do God's will. Contrary to popular belief, God's word is the judge for how well you have been obedient. "As for the person who hears my words but does not keep them, I do not judge him. For I did not come to judge the world, but to save it. There is a judge for the one who rejects me and does not accept my words; that very word which I spoke will condemn him in the last day" (John 12: 47-48). If you say you are his child, you will live as a child of God obeying his words with urgency.

Since spirituality comes from within, the changes that you make inwardly will manifest outwardly in your behavior and speech. "You, however, are not controlled by the sinful nature but by the Spirit if the Spirit of God lives in you. And if anyone does not have the Spirit of Christ, he does not belong to Christ.

But if Christ is in you, your body is dead because of sin, yet your spirit is alive because of righteousness" (Romans 8: 9-10). If you are controlled by your thoughts, wishes and desires as you once were, then the Spirit of God is not in you. It is important in your relationships that you stand firm on your beliefs and make God's word the standard for your life. In every opportunity you encounter, you must make certain you are a spiritual woman not misrepresenting who and what you say you are.

Living as a spiritual woman takes a concerted effort on your part. Prayer will provide guidance and taking careful steps will ensure that you remain on the path of righteousness. Do not compromise God's word. The only way to succeed in pleasing God is to urgently strive to do His Will regardless of the consequences. God will protect you and help you stay focused if you just simply ask Him.

God wants you to be a spiritual woman, upright and holy in every way. "Create in me a pure heart, O God, and renew a steadfast spirit within me" (Psalms 51: 10). He wants to make your heart pure and give you a spirit of love, gentleness, humbleness, and pureness, the very qualities your future mate will be looking for in a woman of God. You must show God that you want this too, by changing the things in your life that prevent this transformation to take place. "Do not merely listen to the word, and so deceive yourselves. Do what it says" (James 1:22).

3

BELIEF

God does have some one special for you, and believing this is the first step to building your faith in God. God has the power to do all things. "Yours, O Lord, is the greatness and the power and the glory and the majesty and the splendor, for everything in heaven and earth is yours. Yours, O Lord, is the Kingdom; you are exalted as head over all" (1 Chronicles 29: 11). Realizing that God is great and has the power to do all things will strengthen your belief in Him. You must believe in God's greatness before you can trust and rely on Him to meet your needs. You are the God who performs miracles; you display your power among the peoples" (Psalms 77:14).

Trust

Without a belief in God's ability and your potential, you will never achieve the things you want because of your fear to trust. Trusting means 'letting go' regardless of your circumstances or current situations. Ask yourself if you are capable of trusting. After thinking about it, most of you will likely trust at least one person, even if that is only yourself. To trust one is to believe that you can rely and depend on them. "Trust him at all times, O people; pour out your hearts to him, for God is our refuge" (Psalms 62:8).

You must learn to depend on God, because He is your

4

only true source of comfort. Believing this will help you gain an understanding of what it takes to relate to others that may end up as potential mates. Trusting completely in God and allowing Him to guide you is the way for you to experience His love and others. "Trust in the Lord with all your heart and lean not on your own understanding; in all your ways acknowledge him, and he will make your paths straight" (Proverbs 3:5-6).

Taking matters into your own hands is not exactly trusting Him. Placing focus on what is believable and what is unbelievable to you is not trusting Him either. You can never understand God's greatness, but you can realize and accept that nothing is too difficult for Him. He has the power to do things unimaginable. Limiting God is saying to Him, "This problem is too big for you, God."

Let go and learn to trust Him for all your needs. Accept Him in all his goodness and have faith that He will meet your needs. "And without faith it is impossible to please God because anyone who comes to him must believe that he exists and that he rewards those who earnestly seek him" (Hebrews 11:6).

FAITHFULNESS

Faithfulness is oftentimes regarded as the way in which you think. Faith defined is confident belief and trust. It is a clear understanding and knowledge that something will happen. "Now faith is being sure of what we hope for and certain of what we do not see" (Hebrews 11:1). God has plans for you but you must remain faithful, because God operates on His time, not yours.

Having a conversation with God daily in good and bad times will build your faith in Him. This will teach you to depend on Him and have faith that He is listening. Faith is a certainty that God will do what He has promised to you. "Know that your Lord God is God; he is the faithful God, keeping his covenant of love to a thousand generations of those who love him and keep his commands" (Deuteronomy 7:9). In times of struggle and suffering, as humans, you get weary and your faith decreases. By speaking with God daily through prayer and study, your faith will increase. Learning to be patient will grant you an opportunity to hear what God wants to say in response to what you have prayed about. "But my righteous one will live by faith. And if he shrinks back, I will not be pleased with him" (Hebrews 11:38).

You must be patient, remain faithful and wait on Him. Praying daily to God and studying His word will teach you the patience you need.

Prayer

Pray daily. Prayer is as essential to life as breathing. "...The prayers of a righteous man are powerful" (James 5:16). Your faith will be tremendously increased if you talk with God on a daily basis. Having a conversation with God should be as

6

natural as having a conversation with your friends. God desires to be a part of your life daily. He wants to hear from you, not only when He is your last resort, but also when things are great in your life. He wants to celebrate your joys and mourn with you during your sorrows. "The Lord is my strength and my shield: my heart trusts in him and I am helped. My heart leaps for joy and I will give thanks to him in song." (Psalms 28:7) Allow Him to be a shepherd over your life, thereby revealing His perfect plan for you. Through prayer, your faith will grow and then you can experience God's uncompromising love.

Study

Study is different from reading. Reading is often times used for enjoyment purposes or knowledge attainment. Studying is to apply one's mind purposefully in order to gain knowledge or understanding of a subject.

Studying God's word is mandatory when building your faith. "Consequently, faith comes from hearing the message, and the message is heard through the word of Christ" (Romans 10:17). What better way to know the great things God is capable of doing for you than by studying His greatness in the scriptures. God allowed His Son to perform miracles daily and He desires to perform them for you. "For God so loved the world that he gave his one and only Son, that whoever believes in him shall not perish but have eternal life" (John 3:16). God wants happiness for you, but you must put Him first. "Delight yourself in the Lord and he will give you the desires of your heart" (Psalms 37:4).

God wants to give you so much, but you are a woman of little faith. "Consider how the lilies grow. They do not labor or spin. Yet I tell you, not even Solomon in all his splendor was dressed like one of these. If that is how God clothes the grass of the field, which is here today, and tomorrow is thrown into the fire, how much more will he clothe you, O you of little faith" (Luke 12: 27-28)! You are afraid to totally rely on Him. Be faithful, trust God, study his word, and let Him show you what having a little faith will do for your life.

Patience

After you pray to God you must wait on Him. "I waited patiently for the Lord; he turned to me and heard my cry" (Psalms 40:1) You must have faith that in time He will provide answers to your questions, present solutions to your problems, and provide assistance when you are in need. God answers prayers, but He operates on His time and not yours. This is repeated because it is important for you to understand that your time *is* God's time; therefore, you must wait on Him. "Yet the Lord longs to be gracious to you; he rises to show you compassion. For the Lord is a God of justice. Blessed are all who wait on him" (Isaiah 30:18)!

Patience will help you determine if and when you are

hearing from God. God knows the plans He has for you. Praying specifically for what you want is advised, but God knows what is best for your life. Therefore, it is wise to focus on aligning your desires with His plans. What if your desires are different from his plans? "Wait for the Lord; be strong and take heart and wait for the Lord" (Psalms 27:14). Attempting to assist Him will oftentimes prolong blessings that He had in store for you.

Lastly, once you have presented a problem or request to God, be at peace knowing that He heard your prayer and will meet your needs as long as you are seeking to do His will. This does not mean that it is unnecessary to pray repeatedly for the things you desire, but know that God heard your requests and is eager to bless you when you are obedient. "Therefore I tell you, whatever you ask for in prayer, believe that you have received it, and it will be yours" (Mark 11:24).

Chapter **2**

CAN YOU RELATE?

"A cheerful heart is good medicine, but a crushed spirit dries up the bones."

Proverbs 17:22

Relating is interacting with others in a meaningful way. If you have not mastered the art of relating to others, then you will find it even more difficult to relate to a mate. Ask yourself these questions to determine if you can relate effectively?

11

- Do you take into consideration the words you choose?

- Are you calm or anxious when speaking?

- Do you respond to others in a positive way?

- Are you effectively expressing what you are relaying?

- Does the listener understand your intention?

- Do you allow the listener to respond?

There are classes on gardening, writing and even how to train a pet, but to my knowledge no class exists on how to relate to the human species. If you answered "no" to two or more of these questions, then there is a desperate need for you to enroll in your first relationship course. Welcome to RELATIONSHIPS 101!

Relationships are high on the list of things people most desire, but there are few opportunities to learn how to be in one. Therefore, the only valid education you receive is the lesson you learn after the relationship has ended. Without an understanding of how to relate to others, you will never have successful relationships. God will not provide you with a mate if you do not know how to relate to others in a manner that is pleasing to him.

What is a relationship?

A relationship is an association between two or more

people. Relationships change over time both positively and negatively. The key to making relationships work begins with *you*.

Do you realize that you can control most of the problems you encounter? You have the ability to influence any situation and make it a positive outcome or a negative outcome. Oftentimes, sadly, you negatively impact those relationships where men are concerned. The desire to be a wonderful friend, mate, and companion is clearly the mission in the beginning of the relationship, but slowly fades– eventually deteriorating; which can ultimately end the relationship.

Male and female relationships are simple. It is important to view them as such. If you learn to appreciate the opportunity to grow daily with another individual, you will become better prepared for the differences that *will* occur in the relationship. Understanding that relationships transform or go through various stages will help you get through these time periods with ease. Inconsistencies within a relationship are foundational and vital to the growth, depth and extent of the relationship. Unbelievably, disagreements are an important building block to relationship development and in addition a free opportunity to do something special for your mate to make up!

To take a closer look at relationships, it is important to understand the dynamics associated with them. There are five main areas that need to be addressed to make any relationship work. These are love, acceptance, compromise, patience and communication.

Love

    Love God first, then yourself, and the love you have for others will shine through because of your love for God. In dealing with others love will help you approach people and situations differently. "Let love and faithfulness never leave you; bind them around your neck, write them on the tablet of your heart" (Proverbs 3:3).

    "What a man desires is unfailing love..." (Proverbs 19:22). Everyone desires to be loved whether that means by family, friends or that special mate that God has for that person. "Love is patient, love is kind. It does not envy it does not boast, it is not proud. It is not rude, it is not self-seeking, it is not easily angered, it keeps no record of wrongs" (1 Corinthians 13: 4-5). If you keep this in mind when you relate to others, God will be pleased and you will build deeper more meaningful relationships.

    When you love someone, it is evident in everything you do and say. In the book of Genesis, Abraham's love for God was obvious. God tested Abraham. "Then God said, 'Take your son, your only son, Isaac, whom you love, and go to the region of Moriah. Sacrifice him there as a burnt offering on one of the mountains I will tell you about' " (Genesis 22:2). The Bible speaks of how urgent Abraham obeyed God. The next morning Abraham began his journey to seek the mountain in which to give his son's life as a sacrifice to God. He was obedient to God and urgent about fulfilling God's request. God loves obedience and He will reward you if you do not hesitate to obey Him.

    Upon Abraham's arrival where God led him, he made preparations to slay his son. At that point with the knife in his hand God spoke to Abraham. *"Do not lay a hand on the boy*, he said. *Do not do anything to him. Now I know that you fear God, because you have not withheld from me your son, your only son"* (Genesis 22:12). He was obedient to God willing to give his only son because of the love he has for God. This type of love is what you must have for God. Nothing God asks of you is too much. After all God gave his son for you and there is nothing you can do to repay Him. Being obedient will only show Him how grateful you are for his love. Are you willing to sacrifice your life for God?

There are many stories of love in the Bible because love is what identifies you as a child of God. "A new command I give you: Love one another. As I have loved you, so you must love one another. By this all men will know that you are my disciples, if you love one another" (John 13:34-35). Love is the basis of most relationships, but it is not all that is needed to make a relationship work. If you say you love someone you accept them for who they are.

Acceptance

Acceptance is the first step in being in a relationship. Acceptance, simply stated, is receiving with gladness. Receiving with gladness means accepting others for who they are at that moment and being totally and completely open with your heart in receiving them. "Accept one another, then, just as Christ accepted you, in order to bring praise to God" (Romans 15:7).

Satisfaction is different from acceptance. We often times confuse the two. Satisfaction involves fulfilling a desire.

Acceptance is receiving regardless of whether the desire is fulfilled or not. Think for a moment about the person that you would most like to be with. Are you accepting the person for who they are or are you attempting to fulfill a desire? You cannot and will not ever be in a successful relationship if you are satisfying yourself rather than accepting the individual.

Satisfaction in a deeper sense means pleasure derived from the gratification of a need or desire. To seek satisfaction is not to accept. There is a distinct difference between individuals who enter relationships with the desire to accept others for who they are and those who desire to satisfy the need to be with someone.

If the latter phase is true, then satisfaction would mean that the person would have to measure up to some standard that you have internally, unconsciously created. Unconsciousness involves that part of the mind that operates without conscious awareness and that cannot be directly observed. This means you may, or may not be aware of the demands you place upon others because of your desire to fulfill a void. Demands are actually restrictions that you place on a potential relationship. This happens often because of your perception of how relationships should be and not how they can be.

Some of the most obvious restrictions that are placed on relationships are age, height, weight, and also race. Some restrictions that are even less obvious but more profound are restrictions such as employment, educational status, living situation and automobile type. What does the type of car one drives have to do with whether or not that person can bring you more joy than you have ever experienced in your life? Do not let this immature selfish thinking be the reason you never experience marriage, raise a family and enjoy the happiness God wants for your life.

It is your unconsciousness that not only leads you to unhealthy relationships, but also that make you stay in them. There are unions that you have chosen to remain a part of that meet, pass and exceed your Relationship Requirement Scale (RRS) with flying colors but are far from the type of relationships you truly desire.

After you have wasted valuable time nurturing a relationship that is unwanted, you begin to adjust the numbers on your scale. You should get rid of your RRS and ask God to help you accept others as they are just as he accepts you as you are. "Rich and poor have this in common: The Lord is the Maker of them all" (Proverbs 22:2). If you use this as the basis of each relationship opportunity you encounter, you would be less likely to submit to your unconscious thinking. This kind of thinking leads you to believe that one must measure up to your pre-selected standard. It is that very thinking that is the core of your unhappiness.

Accepting an individual for what you see and not what you would like to see is not always easy. It involves active participation and a conscious effort on your part at all times until you have mastered the art of accepting others. To master something is to overcome or subdue it. You must *subdue* the thoughts that one should measure up to your standard and *overcome* the idea that until you find this type of individual you will be alone.

You cannot and will not find your mate. "But seek first his kingdom and his righteousness, and all these things will be given to you as well" (Matthew 6:33). Trust God to give you the type of person you deserve to have in your life and show yourself approved by being obedient to his word.

17

Compromise

✳   Compromising with your mate, as long as it does not interfere with being obedient to God, is essential to the growth of the relationship. Since a relationship consists of two or more people, it is important that you take into consideration another's point of view. The reason it is sometimes difficult for you to compromise with others is because for the majority of your life, it has just been you. You make your own decisions about what you do, where you want to go and who you choose to accept into your life. Consequently, you do not know much about compromise, but it is compromise that will lead you to better relationships.

Society encourages fascination with the idea of self, and humans respond selfishly in everything they do. People first consider themselves, before they consider the next person. In considering another human being, you must have regard for his needs and feelings. "Each of you should look not only to your own interests, but also to the interests of others" (Philippians 2:4). Just as you are pleased when others take your feelings into consideration, you must treat others the way you desire to be treated. It is an issue of love and respect; without these your relationship will not get through the early stages. Learn to consider others' feelings, desires and choices.

✳   A wise woman understands that the opportunity to be with a man of God is a gift unlike any other. It is an opportunity to establish a relationship built on love, trust and commitment using the Holy Bible as the standard. Understanding this should better equip you for consciously thinking of how truly blessed you will be once

God allows that man to come into your life.

In any relationship you give and receive. Women often *give* in relationships much more than they ever receive. This is because you think that giving will maintain the relationship. Compromising your value system does not mean you give or buy things for someone in order to gain their interest. Also, never allow a man to disrespect you. Giving will not lead you to a road of happiness and buying him things will not make him love you.

However, compromising God's word means you are choosing to do things that are totally against his will for your life. He will bless you if you choose to let his will and not your will be the basis on which you act, speak and behave. "The acts of the sinful nature are obvious: sexual immorality, impurity, debauchery; idolatry and witchcraft; hatred, discord, jealousy, fits of rage, selfish ambition, dissensions, factions and envy; drunkenness, orgies and the like. I warn you, as I did before, that those who live like this will not inherit the kingdom of God" (Galatians 5:19-21). To compromise God's word for a relationship is to your detriment. "It is the Lord your God you must follow, and him you must revere. Keep his commands and obey him; serve him and hold fast to him" (Deuteronomy 13: 4).

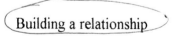

Building a relationship

In order to build something, a foundation is needed. *"Therefore everyone who hears these words of mine and puts them into practice is like a wise man who built his house on the rock.*

19

The rain came down, the streams rose, and the winds blew and beat against that house; yet it did not fall, because it had its foundation on the rock. But everyone who hears these words of mine and does not put them into practice is like a foolish man who built his house on the sand. The rain came down, the streams rose, and the winds blew and beat against that house, and it fell with a great crash" (Matthew 7:24-27). Foundation is actual groundwork. What groundwork is needed to make relationships work? There are not many tools needed, but much patience, understanding and communication are needed to build great relationships.

Patience

One important building block needed is patience. Patience is enduring with calmness. With every moment, incident and occurrence, be patient. Do not be quick to judge, make assumptions or correct any situation. Many times what could have been resolved has been interrupted because patience was not exercised. It is important to listen to the other person in order to get their point of view and opinion of the situation. You already know your own views, expectations, and thoughts; try to focus on what others are feeling.

Communication

Another significant building block is communication. It is the glue that holds a relationship together or the shears that shred it apart. It involves two, not one dominating person monopolizing a

20

conversation. Effective communication can only take place when two individuals are willing to actively participate in the translation of information. Venting, expressing anger, or releasing are not forms of proper communication, because these forms usually involve one speaker that is unable and unwilling to communicate because of unresolved issues and feelings. "Be joyful in hope, patient in affliction, and faithful in prayer" (Romans 12:12). It is not wise to have a conversation when you are unwilling to respond with love and kindness. Pray to God for peace about the situation and then attempt to speak with the other person when you are able to act in a Godly manner.

Proper communication is taking place when an exchange of information is given by a speaker, you, and a listener, the other person. Communication is not occurring unless the other person is relaying information also. Their acknowledgment will be displayed in forms such as a nod or expressing agreement or disagreement. In other words your previous yelling matches were not effective then, and they will not be effective now. Comments from the other person allow you to know how they feel about what you are saying and will let you know if they understand the information you are relaying.

Love, acceptance, patience, compromise and communication are the ingredients needed to begin your life of new and exciting relationships. Practice these daily and you will learn to love unconditionally, communicate with patience, never compromise God's word and accept him and others into your heart always.

Lord help me in these areas, I need your guidance. The spirit is willing but the flesh is sometimes weak. amen.

21

Chapter **3**

...AND SHE SHALL BE CALLED WOMAN

The Lord God said, "It is not good for the man to be alone. I will make a helper suitable for him."

Genesis 2:18

A confident, spiritual woman of God will hold her head high, walk with grace and charm and always exemplify that which is good. She is loving and gentle, kind but firm, and never compromises God's word. She is humble, not prideful...a joy to be around. She lives her life in such a way that if every woman were like her, every life like hers ---this world would be God's paradise. But on the other hand "Like a gold ring in a pig's snout is a beautiful woman who shows no discretion" (Proverbs 11: 22).

Just as there are ways to speak when interacting with others, there are ways a woman of God should act and behave. Manner, is the way or style of doing; and manners are socially proper behavior. In this chapter we are going to discuss both, the way you do things and ways to do them properly in a social setting; but most importantly in a manner that will please God. God made woman to serve as a helpmate for man. If women could embrace this concept, life would be less disappointing and more enjoyable. Women do not fully understand their role according to the word of God. You must know your role before you can carry it out. The misconception that men are the *problem* must be dismissed and the focus and attention must be on self. When this realization takes place, your attention and focus will be on making changes in your own character to the point that you will fail to take note that God has blessed you with a godly man to love and lead you.

Unfortunately for most women, it takes years and many disappointing relationships before you seek God. "Ask and it will be given to you; seek and you will find; knock and the door will be opened to you" (Matthew 7:7). Since you are reading this book, you have finally decided to seek assistance and do things God's way and not your way. The rule of thumb is, 'If I pray to change I will change...and with each change I make I am growing into the woman God wants me to be.' This attitude, studying God's word, prayer

24

and a few outward modifications and soon you will be enjoying the blessing of being in a wonderful relationship with a loving, spiritual man of God.

Spiritual Woman (*inward appearance*)

Personality is the totality of distinctive traits of an individual that make them socially appealing. A Godly woman has a pleasant personality and strives daily to please God by continuously changing. Since change begins on the inside, the thoughts and behavior patterns once learned by you must be replaced with scriptural knowledge. This knowledge is what helps you grow and forces you to change from the inside out. Your focus will be on dying to self and becoming pure in God's sight. "Blessed are the pure in heart, for they will see God" (Matthew 5:8). You will change and others will notice that you have a more positive attitude and loving demeanor. Overall, your attitude must be that you will do anything for God. He does everything for you and you must show him how grateful you are for his love. You can do nothing without Him, but everything with Him. "It is God who arms me with strength and makes my way perfect" (2 Samuel 12:33). God asks so little of you. If you make the first step to being a changed woman by opening your heart and being obedient to His word, he will help you take the rest of them.

Let go, trust God with your heart and allow Him to make you a beautiful, spiritual woman of God on the inside. God judges the heart. "But the Lord said to Samuel, 'Do not consider his appearance or his height, for I have rejected him. The Lord does

25

not look at the things man looks at. Man looks at the outward appearance, but the Lord looks at the heart" (1 Samuel 16:7).

Physical Woman (*outward appearance*)

Change, on the inside, is a decision to allow the word of God to give you convictions about your heart---but outward change involves physical and mental effort. There is an adage that says women are God's gift to men. If this were totally true, you would all be married and living happily ever after. *Not correct.* It is important to be a woman first before you can call yourself God's gift to men. A woman is gentle, soft, and tender. Everything about her is feminine.

Femininity encompasses those qualities that are woman-like. It includes the way you speak, dress, and behave. Dress is not an important factor in being identified as a woman. Women of today are obviously not expected to be clothed in hoop skirts and ankle length dresses, but as today's society may misinform you, you are to look like a w-o-m-a-n.

What does this mean? Looking like a woman is knowing confidently that when a human being from any race, religion, nationality or ethnicity sees you, they know you are without a doubt a female. "A woman must not wear men's clothing, nor a man wear women's clothing, for the Lord detests anyone who does this" (Deuteronomy 22:5).

Certainly there are times when women want to dress casual. A baseball cap is not labeled as inappropriate; but to have the overall appearance of 'one of the boys' is not acceptable. For further instruction on outward appearance please refer to the Appendix.

26

...And she shall be called woman

[handwritten: Thank you Father that you made me woman]

You are a woman because God decided this is the way He wanted it to be. "Then the Lord God made a woman from the rib he had taken out of the man, and he brought her to the man. The man said, 'This is now bone of my bones and flesh of my flesh; she shall be called 'woman,' for she was taken out of man." (Genesis 2:22-23).

[handwritten: Help me God fufill this daily!]

As a godly woman, you are expected to present yourself as a spiritual woman at all times. Women are to act, behave, sit, respond, laugh, joke, play, dance and speak like *women*. Therefore, it is not in God's plan for you to compete with men physically, professionally or in the home. It is of God's choosing that he made you different from men. [handwritten: amen!] You bring beauty to the world and are basically expected to be ultra-feminine cutie pies---at all times.

At all times includes in the store, at a football game and even in the privacy of your own home. Being a woman comes naturally for some of us and it takes work for [handwritten: amen!] many others. Here are three ways to perfect your womanly ways.

ALWAYS, ALWAYS:

- Walk like a lady.
- Speak like a lady.
- Behave like a lady. [handwritten: AMEN for That]

If you can get these three down, you will have mastered the art of womanhood.

[handwritten: Got It!]

27

"Have I not commanded you? Be strong and courageous. Do not be terrified; do not be discouraged, for the Lord your God will be with you wherever you go" (Joshua 1:9).

Walking

Walking is done quite frequently during the day, therefore, if you are walking like a lady your attention will be focused on 'being a lady' for the majority of your waking hours. Eventually, being a lady will be second nature to being a human being.

You should walk gracefully, moderately paced, arms relaxed, body straight and head up. Your steps are firm and your eyes are pointed in the direction in which you are going. You are confident and this confidence is detected by *him* a mile away. Your stature is upright like a tree and you are assured of your ability to handle any situation. This is how a woman of God walks gracefully, confidently and assuredly at all times. Help me Lord to always represent you as such and

Speaking

A godly woman's speech is gentle and soothing. Loud, boisterous speech and knee slapping behavior is not the way a woman of God behaves. Your words are chosen with care and your body is relaxed. Your voice is never raised, but the confidence in your tone shows that you are not afraid to voice your opinion. Lord Help me to maintain the balance needed in this important area of my spiritual growth. Thank you Father for answering my 28 prayer amen!

Your speech flows freely and you are humble enough to not offend others.

A godly woman has no excuse for being unsure about who she is, and this assuredness should always be demonstrated when speaking. You are to be confident that what you say is understood and well received by others. *Lord Help me to first master this as I master it, others will see me as you see me. amen*

Behavior

Lastly, your behavior should not be extreme or severe. Everything about you should be moderate, especially your behavior. There should be a balance. Do not be anxious or reclusive. To others, your personality should be a calm one with an added touch *important word.* of zeal. Your overall demeanor should be somewhat mysterious. Self disclosure should be a step wise approach sharing more revelations as you get to know one another.

God revealed himself slowly to the Israelites. It is wise to let people get to know you gradually; besides, men enjoy the challenge of finding out the unknown. Their interest will increase rather than diminish if you allow them to get to know you slowly.

amen. But Lord Help, Help, Help, me to see the special man of God and respond to him in this way, not the way I'm used to be with my male friends. I want to give him something special that my male friends in the past didn't see, so Lord do you work on me, train me, purge me, renew me in this crucial area of friendship, that's my earnest plea amen.

29

Chapter 4

DATING

"Dear children do not let anyone lead you astray..."

1 John 3:7

There are many ways to do many things, especially date. Only two are going to make all the difference in the world---the right or the wrong way. Dating is not specifically addressed in the Bible, but some Bible commentators believe that dating is for the expressed intent of marriage. To get to know someone my belief is that you must date them, therefore dating righteously must be addressed. With the understanding that you are not going to date now as you did in the world, there is a need to explore ways to date and receive the results you really want--- healthy, happy, spiritual relationships.

Dating provides many wonderful opportunities. It is a chance to meet another human being where an opportunity to build a friendship becomes available. The Webster dictionary defines it as a chance to meet socially. It provides an occasion for social relations that can grow into a friendship that can last a lifetime, a very short time or be destroyed even before it has the chance to develop. How you approach situations while dating will determine how long the potential relationship can last. Making decisions without seeking advice can ultimately be the cause of the disappointments you face while attempting to simply get to know another individual. To turn those social meeting opportunities, or dates, into true meaningful relationships, it is important to set goals, boundaries, and limitations. *I truly understand and agree!*

Goals will assist you in determining what to expect from the date and what to gain from the potential friendship--and ladies, do not let your primary goal be to make this person yours for the rest of your life. Allow the man to lead. It is important for you to make realistic goals. These are goals which can be reached by your efforts *important point again* alone and do not include changing or influencing the way someone else feels about you. Remember this is a chance to build a relationship with a new friend, not an opportunity to determine if he wants to stay in the city or move to a small town and raise three

32

children. A great friendship precedes any healthy relationship.

Dating God's way is different from any dating you probably have experienced before. A date is just a date. It is not to be misinterpreted for the first step to finding the mate of your dreams. *[handwritten: This is my master Lord!]* Remember the first step is building a relationship with God. Dating should be fun and stress-free. An attempt to impress your date in hopes that he will find that he cannot live without you will not take place on date #1. And if there is any possibility of having a second date with him, it would be wise to be yourself, relax and focus on having a good time. Subsequently, if this is your mate, then he will be pleased with your ability to be yourself. If not, you will have had a great time anyway.

To date righteously means you interact with others in a manner that pleases God. Flirting, sending mixed signals and inappropriate touching is not the way a Godly woman behaves. "But among you there must not even be a hint of sexual immorality, or of any kind of impurity, or of greed, because these are improper for God's holy people" (Ephesians 5:3). *[handwritten: Help me Lord to put these into practical. amen]*

Approaching relationships as if there are no 'rules' is a certainty that your possible future relationship will be no more than another bad experience. Doing things the 'right' way will yield positive results, just as doing things the wrong way will yield negative ones. It is imperative to respond to people differently than you did in the past. "As obedient children, do not conform to the evil desires you had when you lived in ignorance" (1 Peter 1:14). With practice this will come naturally, and over time you will be on the road to dating successfully and making friends in ways you never imagined before. How do you date righteously? "Do not be yoked with unbelievers. For what do righteousness and wickedness have in common? Or what fellowship can light have with darkness? What harmony is there between Christ and Belial? What does a believer have in common with an unbeliever? What agreement is there between the temple of God and idols? For we are the temple of the living God. As God has said, "I will live with them and walk among them, and I will be their God, and they will be my people" (2 Corinthians 6:14-16). Date only those men that are like-minded, those that share your feelings about God's word. This means that as a spiritual woman of God, you are to be yoked only with spiritual men. Yoked means married to, in relation with, or dating only men that have the same beliefs as you do. *Send me a godly man after your own heart Lord!*

As a woman living for God, it is your duty to obey *and* everything God's word says. His words are clear and state specifically how He feels about everything He desires for your life. God will not bless anything that goes against His teachings, and that includes blessing any relationship that is not built on His word. God makes it perfectly clear that it is impossible to have a relationship with another individual that does not share your beliefs. If you want God to bless your relationship, you must not compromise His word when it comes to dating. *agreed!*

Some of you will attempt to convince yourselves that the guy you are seeing does share your belief. Attending church service occasionally and knowing one of the Ten Commandments 'Thou

34

shalt not steal', is not even a remote indication that he shares your beliefs. How do you determine if a man believes in God, shares your belief, and is committed to making Jesus Lord and Savior over his life? Be prepared ladies, because this question will leave many of you without a date this Saturday night.

A Godly man:

1. Reads his Bible daily.
2. Studies the Word daily.
3. Prays consistently.
4. Seeks God's approval at all times.
5. Obeys God's word.

"Blessed is the one who reads the words of the prophesy, and blessed are those who hear it and take to heart what is written in it, because the time is near" (Revelation 1: 3).

1. Reading God's word on a daily basis allows him to know what God has to say. A man who knows what God says will be able to share with you what God has to say about your relationship. There will be times that you will need his support, and it will be comforting to know that he is able to

give assistance because of his knowledge of the scriptures. How can he lead you if he does not know what God's word says?

Dating a godly man will provide you with comfort that he is giving you advice according to what the God says and not what he thinks and feels.

2. Reading God's word allows him to know what the Word of God says, but studying it opens his heart to be challenged by God's words. When he studies God's word, he will be able to see the areas in his life that need improvement and he will be able to apply what he studies to both of your lives. . Understanding that we are all sinful from birth, he can see how studying the Word daily will help him grow in those areas where he is weak. Change will take place, and ultimately he will continue to grow into the man God wants him to be. As he is growing, you will grow also.

"The Lord detests the sacrifice of the wicked, but the prayer of the upright pleases him" (Proverbs 15: 8).

3. Praying to God is how you speak to Him, and reading the Bible is how He speaks to you. If you do not have a man

that knows how to pray and prays daily, then you are being led by a man that relies on his own thinking.

Prayer is essential to growth. It is the way for him to have a conversation with God. He wants to help each of His children with their struggles and to meet their needs. A man who prays to God daily will be able to build a relationship with God, therefore will seek guidance from God about the plans He has for his life and yours. God wants to guide His children so that your lives on this earth can be filled with peace and joy. Show Him you are thankful for His love and mercy. Pray and study daily because these are important and will train both of you to rely on God for everything.

"Trust in the Lord with all your heart and lean not on your own understanding; in all your ways acknowledge him and he will make your paths straight" (Proverbs 3: 5-6).

4.   It is a wise man who seeks God's approval. This will ensure that he makes every effort to do and say everything to please God. A man who is striving to do everything that is pleasing to God, will make sure he is pleasing you as well. "Do your best to present yourself to God as one approved, a workman who does not need to be ashamed and who correctly handles the truth" (2 Timothy 2:15).

His love for God will directly affect you. He will respect you as a spiritual woman, which means he will be honest, express love and have high regard for your happiness and more importantly your spiritual growth. He will not be afraid to admit when he has made a mistake, or hesitate to correct you when you are wrong.

Jesus replied, "If anyone loves me, he will obey my teaching. My father will love him, and make our home with him. He who does not love me will not obey my teaching. These words you hear are not my own; they belong to my Father who sent me" (John 14: 23-24).

5.   His obedience to God's word is what will show you if he is whom he claims to be. It is good to read and study God's word, but without obedience, it is useless for change. It is evident when a man has chosen Jesus as Lord over his life because doing God's will is priority in his life. He will have confidence in the scriptures and change his ways with urgency. His obedience will be demonstrated through his behavior. A Godly man obeys urgently, changes immediately and relies on God to do the rest.

Now that you know how to determine if a man is godly, it is imperative that you evaluate your present situations and circumstances. Basically, you need to separate yourself from those that did not pass the test. God's word says He will not bless a relationship that is unequally yoked. Are you presently in a relationship that is impure or unholy? If so, free yourself from this unspiritual union and ask God to bless you with a man that will love you the way God wants you to be loved. Thank you Lord, for your covering over me!

Only God knows when and if you are ready for a mate. Pray for Him to reveal things to you about your relationships and He will answer you. "Submit yourselves, then, to God. Resist the devil and he will flee from you" (James 4:7). Be specific about what it is you would like to know and do this with urgency. Your true mate of a lifetime is waiting on you to get yourself right with God. Oh yeah! So I recieve him w/ open faith arms from you Lord away!

For those of you who think you passed the test, or are just too afraid to face reality pray and do not overlook the warning signs. You can choose to remain in a situation that you are certain will not be blessed by God, one bringing you doubt and never wholly providing security in the relationship or you can make a decision to allow God to work in your life and prepare you for the type of relationship He wants for you.

If you feel that you are ready to date spiritual men of God, be prepared to date like you never have before. Dating pure and holy will lead to future relationships based on friendship first. Send Lord! Your godly man will respect you at all times and be an example for you to

39

follow. Dating 'God's Way' is an opportunity to grow in His word, make friends and have lots of fun. The ten points below will get you started on your way to happy dating, 'God's way'. They are categorized under three headings: before the date, during the date and after the date, to help you learn them with ease.

TEN POINTERS FOR A GREAT DATE

1. Relax

2. Be grateful for the opportunity

3. Be yourself

4. Communicate

5. Let him lead

6. Smile

7. Listen

8. Be an encouragement

9. Be sincere

10. Express thanks and appreciation

Thank you Father for your wisdom, above all things, I will put them into practice. 1/1/05

Before the date

1. Relax

There are many things to do before your date, but relaxing is the most important. Relax your mind and body so that you will be at your best. Relaxing mentally and physically will provide you with the overall calm demeanor that will be needed to have a great time and be totally focused on the date.

Prayer is an excellent way to prepare your mind for the date. Pray that God will be in the midst of everything you do and say. Be committed to being an upright woman of God in your actions, speech and manner. Taking the time to relax your mind will mentally prepare you for the date and ensure that you are at your very best.

Reading, watching a movie or taking a walk are other ways to soothe your mind. These activities will also help you relax and help you to have an enjoyable date.

2. Be grateful for the opportunity

It is a blessing to have the opportunity to make new friends. Remember in order to have friends you must first know how to be a friend. Be grateful that God has given you this chance.

Express gratitude by being kind and courteous throughout

the date because this pleases God. "Consider therefore the kindness and sternness of God: sternness to those who fell, but kindness to you, provided that you continue in his kindness. Otherwise you also will be cut off" (Romans 11:22).

During the date

3.   Be yourself

He is only a man and God made many of them, besides the true you is only two dates away. He asked you on a date because he would like to get to know you better. So be yourself, have a great time getting to know another friend, and let your light shine brightly.

Be careful not to get so involved in being your best that you begin pretending to be someone you are not. On the contrary, if you are an individual who sometimes gets extremely comfortable, and you know who you are, stay focused on being quiet and gentle. Giving him 'high-fives' on the date is a little too relaxed.

Basically, be secure with who you are and confident that you are as worthy as the next person to be given all the things God has for you. Confidence is a very appealing quality and one he is sure to appreciate.

4.   Communicate

Communicate effectively not excessively. Conversation will allow you to get to know each other better. Speak when spoken to, elaborate as little as possible and answer confidently. These are rules that you can use. "Instead, it should be that of your inner self, the unfading beauty of a gentle and quiet spirit, which is of great worth in God's sight" (1 Peter 3:4). Quiet means silent or hushed. You can find out more about him and what he has to say if you practice this technique. It is not important that you tell him your entire life story in one conversation. If he is interested, there will be other opportunities to share and if he is not, then what sense did it make telling him you skinned your knee in sixth grade while climbing on the monkey bars anyway.

Your date will appreciate the opportunity to share things with you about himself, if you follow this pointer. Excessive talking is annoying, not just from you but from anyone. There should be a balance of questions and answers during your conversation with him asking most of the questions. Volunteering too much information will not leave him with many questions to ask. Men love the unknown, let him ask you what he wishes to know about you.

Help Lord me!

5.   Let him lead

Allow him to decide where to go, when to go there and how to get there. Leading is very important to men. Though they would

+ Important Dia

never admit it, being in charge feeds their ego. Allowing him to lead is a way to show him you have confidence in him. It is a sign of respect for him and for the decisions he makes. This kind of respect will not go unnoticed.

To question his ability to lead is an insult to him. Men do not wear their heart on their sleeves, but they have an imaginary notebook in their head. Your job is to make certain that the mental notes he is taking on you, are good ones. Be humble and patient and allow him to take control of the date.

6.   Smile

A smile can mean many different things to your date. It says you are happy to be with him, you are in a good mood and you are having a great time. Smiling will express sincere appreciation for the time spent, and has the ability to brighten any room.

It will mean a lot to him to see you smiling while you are with him ...And besides I am certain if you smile, he will almost always smile back!

7.   Listen

Listening is something you view as a small thing, but it truly is a very big one. If he is concentrating more on how to get a word in than he is about what he is expressing to you, then you are probably talking too much. A woman is more attractive when she

44

is quiet. If you are not talking excessively, he will be able to look at you and appreciate the opportunity of each quiet moment. Sharing is fine, but sharing every passing thought you have had in a two hour time period is not. Men get bored easily. Talking too much is a quick way to loose both his attention and his interest.

HELP LORD me!

Listening is a tool used to build any relationship. Show him that he has your undivided attention and that you are completely focused on what he has to say to you. With hope, at the end of your date you will have done this very well and he will conclude that you are a great listener. If this is his opinion then more than likely he will enjoy having the opportunity to talk with you again.

8.   Be an encouragement

People enjoy hearing good things, especially about themselves. It is an encouragement to receive a compliment or to be told that you are doing something well. A date provides the opportunity to share how much you are enjoying the company of another. Express yourself honestly and openly, but remember to encourage him at the same time.

Simple things encourage men. You can comment on his restaurant selection or the shirt he is wearing, but make certain you find pleasant things to say while out on your date. Remember, you have one opportunity to make a good impression. Do not miss it.

9. Be sincere

Sincerity equals truthfulness. It is not necessary to make a comment just for the sake of being encouraging, but be truthful because he will know if you are being sincere. A sincere comment will be well received by him, just as a fictitious act of kindness will be obvious.

Be open and express your true feelings, but do this kindly and with sincerity.

After the date

10. Express thanks and appreciation

It is the word you learned at the age of two–thanks. Expressing gratitude is the proper way to show him how much you appreciate him sharing his time with you. A man of God will not expect but will appreciate your taking the time to say 'thanks'. A token of your appreciation is not required but it will show him that you took notice in everything he did to make your date an enjoyable one.

If you choose, writing a note of thanks is appropriate. Be sure to make it personal by mentioning something about the date. (ex. I had fun bowling, The ballet was an excellent choice, etc.)

Social gatherings

Women are often invited to special events. With various levels of dining today there are few clear cut rules of etiquette; but there are a few things to remember to ensure that your evening out is a success.

1. Be aware of the dress code. Nothing is more uncouth than arriving at an event only to find that you are improperly dressed. You will be more at ease if you have on proper attire for the event. Be certain to ask questions.

2. Eat before you arrive. A function where there is food served is not an opportunity to eat a free meal. It is there to enjoy while you converse and mingle, not to comment, 'Oh, I'm full', upon finishing.

3. Be friendly

    In the company of his friends, you want to maintain your usual friendly attitude. Talk to others and give compliments as needed. Share in the evening by participating and have conversations with others. Make an effort to fit in with the group, and by all means do not stay attached to him the entire time you are in mixed company. Be assured, he will not leave without you. Just have fun enjoying the evening and when he wants you, he will find you.

Lord this is not my problem but
to say, its the opposite, so
Help me to learn balance when
it comes to people. Thank you
Father that you heard my
prayer and answered it,
amen,

48

CHAPTER **5**

GETTING IT TOGETHER

----

*"We hear that some among you
are idle. They are not busy; they
are busy-bodies."*

(2 Thessalonians 3:11)

49

When entering a relationship it is important that you too bring something to the relationship other than just yourself. Just as you expect a man to be able to care for you, you must also have something to offer. Idleness is ungodly and laziness is a sin. "Besides they get into the habit of being idle and going about from house to house. And not only do they become idlers, but also gossips and busybodies, saying things they ought not to" (1 Timothy 5:13). It is important that before you begin praying for that wonderful mate that you focus on getting yourself together first. A man is likely to prefer a mate who has goals and a plan to achieve those goals.

When you are obedient to God, He will give you with the desires of your heart, but it would be wise for you to know what it is that you desire. Getting yourself together will mean that you know where you are going and that you have a plan to get there. Pursue your impossible dreams and be able to confidently pray to God about them being assured that they will come to pass. Jesus replied, "*What is impossible with men is possible with God*" (Luke 18:27). Nothing is too difficult for God, therefore when He opens a door helping you achieve your dreams, be forceful and put forth your best effort to make the dream an attainable goal and eventually that goal a reality.

You must also be able to determine in your mind how you wish to accomplish each task associated with your goals, therefore you will know what to ask of God. Pray about it daily keeping a journal with a list of all things associated with each particular goal.

50

Eventually you will see that your impossible dream has now become real. Your life will be filled with joy because your mind and heart will be in tune with each other. This joy will help you to have confidence in your abilities and strengthen your faith in God's greatness. You will then begin to experience complete internal peace, because of your faith in God and your visible examples of His love for you.

It is obvious why a man would prefer to be with a woman who knows where she is going. If your life is together, then you will be better prepared to serve as a helpmate to him. Also, it is important that you are able to express your hopes and dreams to your mate. Having stability in your life will allow the two of you to come together and move forward with your lives, assisting each other in accomplishing the things you both desire .

If you are afraid to pursue your goals, then how will you help him pursue his goals? There is no need to fear because God wants you to succeed. He wants what is best for you in all areas of your life. "Observe what the Lord your God requires: Walk in his ways, and keep his decrees and commands, his laws and requirements, as written in the Law of Moses, so that you may prosper in all you do and wherever you go (1 Kings 2:3).

Because of fear many people remain in situations that do not fulfill their desires, while other individuals are not motivated to do anything more with their lives because they are lazy. Whether your excuse is fear or laziness, your potential mate will be disappointed to know that you are uncertain about your future and afraid to pursue your dreams. Since his future is of importance to him, he will be more comfortable knowing that you have a desire to be your best also. If he discovers that you are unable to achieve your own goals, or that you have no goals it can be dissatisfying. This may serve as an indicator to him that you are not the woman for him.

Regardless of the disappointments you face, it is important that you strive to do things that will prepare you for the many experiences life will present. This will make you a better helpmate because you will not flinch when faced with difficulties. Strength is a quality that a man can appreciate in the right situation. Inevitably, you will experience hardships and struggles, but in every situation there is an opportunity to learn something. Be courageous and go after the things you desire to do and become. With God on your side, you cannot lose; you will have only gained more strength for the next challenge life has for you.

Since goals are a desired result or purpose, you must know your purpose. What is your true desire? Why have you not forcefully taken every opportunity to make your goal become a reality? More than likely you have given yourself and others many excuses, otherwise you would have already met that goal and moved on to the next one. There are no acceptable excuses for fear of failure as a child of God. True disciples do not fail, they live and learn from the mistakes they make. "If the Lord delights in a man's way, he makes his steps firm; though he stumble, he will not fall, for the Lord upholds him with his hand" (Psalm 37:24).

God will direct you if you allow him to. He wants you to

achieve all your goals, but you will need to take action once He has placed it in your heart what you need to do. Do not continue to make excuses for not having what you truly desire in life. "I sought the Lord, and he answered me; he delivered me from all my fears." (Psalm 34:4). You must pursue your goals and be confident that God will be with you. "The wicked man flees though no one pursues, but the righteous are as bold as a lion" (Proverbs 28:1).

Lastly, focus is the key to achieving the things you want to achieve. You must look at it, write it and speak it into existence daily. Whatever it is that you desire, then you must put forth an effort daily to ensure that you receive it. You must first have a plan. Your plan will consist of things you feel must take place in order to accomplish this goal. You can do this by making an outline of the tasks needed to complete the goal. Afterwards place a timetable with your outline determining dates that you will have each task complete. Do not move to the next task until that task is finished, then begin focusing on your next goal immediately following.

Though God allows us free will, it is important that you always pray and seek His approval. If it comes easy, it has been said that it means it is of God. Regardless of how simple or difficult it is to accomplish your goals, it should be understood that all your dreams will become reality because of your obedience to God.

You have all that you need to accomplish everything you desire to accomplish in this lifetime. Begin today preparing for your future of unlimited possibilities.

It is to prosper me, Lord help me each day to be obedient to your word and the will for my life, help me to die to myself, putting away idleness, and laziness, help me to continue to seek ye first your kingdom and your righteousness. I know by doing so that all things that's in your will for me you will give to me. give measures, shaken down and running over. amen.

CHAPTER **6**

MARRIED AND ENGAGED

(those pretending to be married)

> *"Better to live in a desert than with an ill-tempered wife."*
>
> Proverbs 21:19

Congratulations!!! You have received what you have been waiting on your entire life. You have arrived –the ring, the white

55

4-26-98

gown and the words, "I do"...and your dream becomes reality.

Now that the lights, camera and action are over, let us get down to business. The business of 'marriage'. A marriage requires love, patience, and understanding all of which I am sure you are handling just fine, ..but the 'S' word is the one that demands attention. Submissiveness is the one that will ensure that you remain happy and in love 'till death do you part' or that you just remain 'married', if you are lucky.

"Wives, submit to your husbands as to the Lord. For the husband is the head of the wife and Christ is the head of the church, his body, of which he is the Savior. Now as the church submits to Christ, so also wives submit in everything" (Ephesians 5:22-24). Submissiveness is a word that has practically been removed from our vocabulary. Women do not often use it, understand or even know the meaning of this word. It is to yield (oneself) to the will or authority of another. Though for most of you, yielding to and accepting authority are not things you were taught as little girls, but it is the source of many women's problems. You are unable to allow a man, or for that matter anyone else, lead you anywhere.

Women submissiveness is the key to success in your marriage--successful happy times and successful disagreements. God allowed this marriage to take place with the hope that you will allow your mate to lead you. It is impossible to lead someone who thinks they have already discovered the most feasible way to do everything. Trust your mate to hear from God and allow him to make decisions for the both of you. After all he loves God; therefore, he loves you. Your mate has your best interest at heart if you would just allow him to show you.

Certainly there will be times that he will make mistakes, just as we all do as human beings. Allow him to correct those mistakes. Attention! For those of you who have the desire to do *something*, spend time thinking of wonderful new ways to praise him after he has corrected his mistake. A godly man desires a woman that is spiritual and submissive and he does not want and will not accept any imitations. You will not find your way to the heart of a man of God without these and many other characteristics.

"Wives, submit to your husband, as is fitting in the Lord" (Colossians 3:18). Submissiveness is humble respect. To respect is to show expressions of consideration and have high regard for something or someone. Men are to be respected at all times. As leaders they are the head. To disrespect your husband is disrespecting God. "...and the wife must respect her husband" (Ephesians 5:33). You must obey everything God has commanded of you and his word states that you are to respect your husband.

God blessed you with a husband and now there are things that He expects you to do in this marriage. Your role is a multi-faceted one. It is a role that can be successfully carried out by you when you take a serious look at what God says about submission. Women disrespect their husbands in many ways. It is important that you show respect for your husband by 1) letting him lead 2) being a helpmate 3) and loving him with all your heart.

Lord please prepare me, I'm open to hear and do that which you have purposed. amah!

Leading

"Now I want you to realize that the head of every man is Christ, and the head of every woman is man, and the head of Christ is God" (1 Corinthians 11:3). It is not fitting for a wife to lead her husband. God has total faith that your husband is able to lead you, and you too must have faith in God and His Word. If you have a man of God as a husband, then there are no excuses for why you should be attempting to lead. Trust in God and God will ensure that your needs are met spiritually, mentally and physically. There is no acceptable reason for your husband to fight for his role as the leader.

Being a helpmate

God blessed you with a husband because he knew that man needed a helpmate. "The Lord God said, 'It is not good for the man to be alone. I will make a helper suitable for him" (Genesis 2: 18). God made you for man, and not man for you. As his helper, you are to assist him doing whatever God has called him to do. Your job as the helper consists of lending support, giving assistance, and improving what he has already set out to do. It also states in Webster's that a helper waits on and serves. Are you serving your husband or do you feel that he is to serve you? You are to serve your husband just as he is to serve you.

To serve is to meet a need. The need your husband most desires to be met is your decision to allow him to be the man and support him in the decisions he makes. As the head your husband must be able to hear from God about matters that concern both of you. God will speak to the head in a marriage and not to you. "For the husband is the head of the wife as Christ is the head of the church, his body, of which he is the Savior. Now as the church submits to Christ, so also wives should submit to their husbands in everything" (Ephesians 5:23-24).

He cannot hear from God if his focus is on listening to you. Give him a chance to lead you by listening to God about the path he needs to take for both your lives. This can be accomplished by him with ease if you are making his life simpler and not more difficult. Be cooperative, not combative, and overall more supportive of the decisions he makes.

Being Loving

Love is an intense affection and warm feeling for another. The way you show others that you love them is simple. You express it either verbally or in your actions. It is displayed in your behavior and how you interact with your husband. Love should not be stagnant. This means if it is given proper attention then it grows deeper and deeper with time. If the love for your husband is not growing deeper and more passionate for your husband, then there is a need for more action on your part. On the next few pages you will find ways to keep your marriage from becoming stagnant.

A stagnant marriage is a union between two very unhappy

people. It is up to you to keep your marriage from becoming this way. "The wise woman builds her house, but with her own hands the foolish one tears it down" (Proverbs 14:1). You have the ability to change things in your marriage by being a different type of wife. This change can take place instantly, but it is up to you to make it happen.

> "A wife of noble character who can find?
> She is worth far more than rubies.
> Her husband has full confidence in her and
> lacks nothing of value.
> She brings him good, not harm,
> all the days of her life" (Proverbs 31:10-12).

Since love is the basis of marriage, this is also how you will remain married. Expressing your love for your husband is a guaranteed way to keep your marriage alive. Loving him in good and bad times is what marriage is all about. The love you have in your heart for him must be expressed to him often and it should be evident by the way you interact with him. Telling him you love him is one thing, but demonstrating it is another.

Certainly verbal expressions of love are good, but words without action are useless. The words "I Love You" are some of the nicest words to hear. This is an excellent way to share your feelings of love if you are a woman who rarely expresses your feelings verbally; but what use would it be for your husband to tell you that he wants what is best for you if he is unwilling to work and provide for you? His words are meaningless because there are no actions that support what he is saying. In the same way, when you say to him that you love him, your actions should support the words. Words without sincere actions to support the statements are useless for growth in any relationship. *Lord help me to not only* ~~*I love you but to show it*~~ *enough*

Our true thoughts and feelings are displayed in our behavior. If you apologize and immediately repeat the same behavior, then your apology becomes meaningless because the action did not follow the words. "For the word of God...judges the thoughts and attitudes of the heart" (Hebrews 4:12). If you are sincere about changing then there is action following the decision. Since words and actions go hand in hand, it is important as married women that you do more action and less talking. Love can be felt by your husband in the things you do, just as you feel his love for you by his actions.

As the nurturer, God holds you responsible for keeping your family together. Love is the basis of a marriage and is of utmost importance to God. "If I speak in tongues of men and of angels, but have not love, I am only a resounding gong or a clanging cymbal. If I have the gift of prophecy and can fathom all mysteries and all knowledge, and if I have a faith that can move mountains, but have not love, I am nothing. If I give all I possess to the poor and surrender my body to the flames, but have not love, I gain nothing" (1 Corinthians 13:1-3). What are your actions of love for your husband?

61

You are to make your husband proud that he has you as his wife. Remember you were made for him. If you think of how life was before you were married, this should help you get focused. Take a moment to think of your life before your husband. Go back to that time when you wanted to be happy and you felt that having someone in your life to love you would make all your dreams come true. Now that you are married, it is your duty to help keep this marriage together. God has blessed you with this and now you must do your part to make it all that He has planned for it to be. Make your husband happy. Be a joy to him and love him with everything that you are.

Disrespecting him is not showing him you love him. "Better to live on the corner of the roof than share a house with a quarrelsome wife" (Proverbs 21:9). Wives, you are to love your husbands, not make their lives difficult. So he forgot your birthday present, did not empty the trash again, and was late picking you up. Is this a reason not to speak to him for three days? "Love is patient, love is kind. It does not envy, it does not boast, it is not proud. It is not rude, it is not self-seeking, it is not easily angered, it keeps no record of wrongs" (1 Corinthians 13:4-5).

A wise woman handles matters with prudence or practicality. "Houses and wealth are inherited from parents, but a prudent wife is from the Lord" (Proverbs 19: 14). Communicating your feelings is the way a Godly woman handles situations. Speak to your husband in a manner that will be well-received by him because this is what is expected of you by God. "Be kind and compassionate to

I pray the law of kindness on my tongue and _____ a bridle over most things which does not edify me amen!

one another, forgiving each other, just as Christ God forgave you" (Ephesians 4: 32). No one is perfect, but God. Your husband will make many mistakes in your marriage, as will you. Take advantage of opportunities to show him that his love is more important to you than the fact that he does not do everything you feel he should. Pray to God about situations that are beyond your control and God will answer your prayers. You will receive a more receptive response to your request if you approach your husband with love verses discontentment.

Of course, there are times when you need to assist him in matters. "What do you prefer? Shall I come to you with a whip, or in love and with a gentle spirit?" (1 Corinthians 4: 21). Be kind, humble, loving and gentle when correcting. "Pleasant words are a honeycomb; sweet to the soul and healing to the bones" (Proverbs 16:24). Your husband will be more receptive to love and humbleness than to rebuke. When speaking to him, preface your requests with loving remarks and encouragement. Pray to God about your concerns and ask him to give you the proper words to say because this will reap positive results.

WAYS TO EXPRESS YOUR LOVE FOR YOUR MATE

1. Tell him you love him EVERYDAY.
2. Be submissive.
3. Be honest and open.
4. Forgive him.

5.   Be encouraging.

6.   Support him.

7.   Let him lead you.

8.   Trust him.

9.   Love him unconditionally.

10.   Be patient with him.

11.   Be gentle.

12.   Meet his needs. (mentally, physically and spiritually)

13.   Do not nag.

14.   Make yourself beautiful for him inside and out.

15.   Listen.

16.   Respect him.

17.   Do not pressure him.

18.   Accept him for whom he is.

19.   Allow him to be right.

20.   Tell him he is the only man in the world for you.

Expectations

Your relationship has the potential to be everything you desire it to be if you communicate effectively and strive to meet each others expectations daily. You expect things from your husband as the leader of your household and he expects things from you. Women oftentimes rely on their hearts whereas men think with their minds. Though he may not always express to you what he presumes should happen, he does have expectations. Here are a few to get you moving in the right direction.

The obvious expectations are respect, love, and honesty. As his helpmate he assumes that you will be patient with him, support and assist him in accomplishing his goals. But whether your hubby is a old-fashioned teddy bear or a high-powered businessman, men want the same thing—a woman who loves him unconditionally, supports and encourages him consistently and gives herself to him wholly. There has been an entire chapter set aside for support and encouraging your mate, so loving him unconditionally will be addressed.

"My command is this: Love each other as I have loved you" (John 15:12). God says that you are to love the way he loves. Do not remind your husband of his faults because God will not remind you of yours. In spite of your shortcomings, misfortunes and sinful nature God still loves you. "for all have sinned and fall short of the Glory of God" (Romans 3:23). The same love God has for you, you are to have for others especially your husband. Being loving is not reminding him of his faults, instead supporting in everything.

As the man and head of the family, your husband has the responsibility of leading you and making sure that his family is being obedient to God's word. This is a difficult task that he finds very challenging at times. It is up to you to uplift him when he is doing this in a manner that you feel is acceptable and when you think he is making mistakes. A man who loves God, prays for assistance and speaks with God about the decisions and choices he makes. Do not use his mistakes as an opportunity to show him his fault. Be loving and supportive at these times. Unconditional love is based on your ability to be there for him in good and bad times. At those moments when he is down, he needs your unconditional love the most.

A man knows when he has made a mistake. It is not necessary for you to tell him, because he is very much aware when he has failed. What he needs is for you to love him in spite of the mistake. Be there for your husband the way you expect him to be there for you. Rather, lift him up when he is disappointed—and he is always disappointed when he does not meet the expectations he places on himself. Do not add stress to this disappointment but reassure him that you love him and that you are always there to support him. He depends on you to be in his corner when he feels no one else is there for him. Meet his expectation and show him how much he means to you by supporting him every opportunity you are given. This will add depth to your relationship and increase the love you have for each other.

When he has made a mistake in the past similar to the one he will make again in the future, do not remind him of it. Leave the past in the past. No one wants to be reminded of their disappointments, including you. There is a future of happiness waiting to be explored so why waste time looking backwards. Focus on ways you can help him improve in those areas where he may be weak. Remember, you are his helpmate. Help him grow while at the same time expressing your unconditional love for him. Show him that you are willing to help him improve, rather than rehash the past. This will deepen his appreciation for you and strengthen the bond between the two of you.

Unconditional love also means expressing your feelings in ways that matter to him. A man expects you to cook for him, keep the house clean and take care of bedroom matters. These are things that he assumes you understood prior to you saying 'I do'. If this was understood previously then why must he requests these things of you now that you are married?

Let us begin with cooking. Yes, women of the nineties, it is expected that you cook a meal for your husband everyday. I am aware that you work and have a schedule that matches his, but he is the sole breadwinner (in most cases) and you are the wife. The man provides and the wife serves. He deserves a home cooked meal everyday, just as you deserve a roof over your head everyday. Do not view this negatively but as another opportunity to express your unconditional love for him.

Keeping the home clean also makes your husband happy. He may not express this to you because it is not as important to him as bedroom matters and cooking, but everyone likes the feeling of cleanliness. Yes, even your husband the one who throws his clothes on the floor and never lifts a hand without your suggestion. It is a sacrifice to maintain a job, raise a family, cook and clean everyday, but it is part of the 'wife' duties you accepted on your special day. Jesus made a sacrifice for you and God blessed you with a husband and you are to make a sacrifice and thank God for that husband. If you make a sacrifice for your husband, he will certainly make a bigger one for you. Men are just that way. They act in response to your actions. You have the ability to have him do exactly what you desire, if you go the extra mile to please him.

Speaking of pleasing him, there is another thing that brings him happiness. And this matter must be addressed. Working women, housewives and all those in between---you must meet your husbands need. Yes, that is the need I am speaking of. He enjoys spending time with you. He needs this special attention like a fish needs water. Please ensure that his tank is never empty. Can you imagine a fish without water? A terrible thing it is. Men should not have to ask to be with you. It is your wifely duty. He should have to tell you that he will catch *you* tomorrow. It is imperative that you provide the intimacy men need and desire. This is his way of showing you that he loves you, and of course an opportunity to perform for you. Do take advantage of these opportunities. It makes him happy to know you want him as much as he wants you. Do not lack in this area ladies, it is to your disappointment if you allow him to get to a comfortable place where this matter is concerned.

Sexual relations between you and your mate provide an opportunity to grow together in a deeper more meaningful way. You have your mate at the most vulnerable place ever when you share with him intimately. To miss any opportunity to grow closer to him at this time will place limitations on your marriage, sexual relationship and ultimately your love for each other.

WOMEN MARRIED TO NON-BELIEVERS

"Wives, in the same way be submissive to your husbands so that, if any of them do not believe the word, they may be won over without words by the behavior of their wives, when they see the purity and reverence of your lives" (1 Peter 3: 1-2). Wives married to unbelievers are placed in a very challenging position, but one that can be blessed tremendously with prayer, faith and perseverence. "For this very reason, make every effort to add to your faith goodness; and to goodness, knowledge; and to knowledge, self-control, perseverance; and to perseverance, godliness;" (2 Peter 1:5). You must always carry yourself in a manner that pleases God, then your husbands will be influenced positively by your behavior. On the other hand, if your lifestyle does not match what you profess to believe, then he will be more inclined to rebel. Do not compromise your standard of living for your husband. You will do a better job of encouraging him to follow God's word by standing firm in you belief than you will by being inconsistent. You can be assured that he is watching everything you do. He wants to know if you believe what you say you believe and how devoted you are to God.

It is difficult living in a situation with a non-believer, in fact, you may be tempted to respond to his actions, be lackadaisical in your study and possibly waiver in your faith. Pray daily. Not only for your husband, but for yourself. Pray that you do not compromise God's word and that your actions are always that of a

Godly woman. Be faithful in your belief that God will do what he has promised. "...The righteous will live by faith" (Romans 1:17). Be confident and know that just as you were saved, your husband can be too.

Do not give up hope that your husband will someday become a God-fearing man. If you are obedient and an example at all times, never compromising God's word, He will bless your efforts. "I am the Lord, the God of all mankind. Is anything too hard for me" (Jeremiah 32:27)? To your surprise, you will eventually see the day that your husband becomes the man of God that you would have him to be.

ENGAGED

At this point most of you have the ring, though there are many of you that do not. Not only do you not have the ring, you probably do not have his word that there will truly be a wedding. Just because he agrees with your idea that the two of you will be married, does not mean that there will actually be a ceremony. Ask yourself whether it was your idea to get married or his. If it is your idea in any form or fashion, then you can save money, time and trips to the bridal shop. He is not going to marry you if he did not suggest it. To make it clearer for those of you wishing to get married, here is a list of ways you will know if you are or are not getting married.

70

YOU MAY NOT BE GETTING MARRIED IF:
---

1. He has not given you a ring.

2. His mother does not know. (*You* or about the wedding)

3. He decided that he would marry you after you threatened to leave him.

4. You and his mother came up with the idea together.

5. You are doing the majority of the planning and he has very little to say about anything.

6. You gave him an ultimatum.

7. He makes excuses. (ex. financial stability, wrong timing)

8. He is still married.

9. You continue to live with him hoping he will eventually come around.

10. You have only remained together because you decided at all costs he is the man for you.

Now for those of you that are still getting married, there are a few things that must be discussed before you make this trip down the aisle. It is important that you know in your heart that it is God's will for you to get married. To get married without God's approval is the start of a very unhappy life for you. You will be *married*--- and that is all. Your marriage will never be what you hope for and desire without God's blessing. Allow him to choose your partner and make you part of a union that will last a lifetime. God wants you to marry the man that He has for you and not the man that you want for yourself. Pray specifically, be patient and listen to God. "For I know the plans I have for you," declares the Lord, "plans to prosper you and not harm you, plans to give you hope and a future. Then you will call upon me and come and pray to me, and I will listen to you. You will seek me and find me when you seek me with all my heart." (Jeremiah 29: 11-13).   *amen*

Ask yourself:

- Is this marriage God's will or my will?
- Is God ready for me to be married as much as I am ready to be married? *please answer me Lord amen*
- As I am today will God send one of his son's to me for me to serve as his wife and helpmate forever? *I pray this father amen*
- Am I striving daily to be the woman of God that God wants me to be? *I need your help father amen*
- Do I understand what it means to submit? *amen*
  Please give me clarity, wisdom and knowledge as to how amen

72

It states in the Bible that women must submit to their husbands. "Wives, submit to your husbands as to the Lord..." (Ephesians 5:22). If the word, submit, is not a household term, then you are not ready for marriage. The man is the head and your role is that of the follower. He hears from God and you hear from your mate. If you are not totally comfortable with being led, then you are not ready to be married.

God knows when it is time for you to become a wife. He has plans for your life and is eager to bless you once you totally submit yourself and your life to Him. "Submit to God and be at peace with him; in this way prosperity will come to you. Accept instruction from his mouth and lay up his words in your heart" (Job 22: 21-22). *Lord I seek your guidance Each day knowing that you will lead me anew*

To experience true happiness, your goal in life must be to do God's will in everything. "For whoever finds me finds life and receives favor from the Lord" (Proverbs 8: 35). He has a plan for you, but it is up to Him as to how he will carry it out. As a woman who understands the importance of being obedient to God, you must love submission because it is God's expectation. "A woman must learn in quietness and full submission. I do not permit a woman to teach or to have authority over a man; she must be silent" (1Timothy 2:11).

If you understand that you are to allow your mate to lead you, then you will inevitably learn to be patient. You will need patience when and if you get married. Also patience is needed in case God decides that this is not the man for you. Only God knows the day you will get married. However, as it is written, "No eye has seen, no ear has heard, no mind has conceived what God has prepared for those who love him" (1 Corinthians 2:9). His plans for your life are worth waiting for. Do not be eager to get married or do anything else without consulting with God. "Do not be anxious about anything , but in everything, by prayer and petition, with thanksgiving, present your requests to God. And the peace of God, which transcends all understanding, will guard your hearts and your minds in Christ Jesus" (Philippians 4: 6-7).

Imagine for a moment that God reveals to you that this is not the man for you. It is important that you take heed to God's warning. Let your goal be to make sure your next relationship does not end up as another disappointment. Now this is what the Lord Almighty says: "Give careful thought to your ways. You have planted much, but harvested little. You eat, but never have enough. You drink, but never have your fill. You put on clothes, but are not warm. You earn wages, only to put them in a purse with holes in it" (Haggai 1: 5-6). Seek God's will your life and have complete confidence in His ability to give you the desires of your heart.

Do not be eager to be in a relationship. Being single is far better than being in a marriage that is not ordained by God. Wait patiently and pray continually about what you desire for God to give you. He is a faithful God and willing to bless you if you fight daily to be the Godly woman he expects you to be. "This is the confidence we have in approaching God: that if we ask anything according to his will, he hears us. And if we know that he hears us–whatever we ask–we know that we have what we asked of him" (1 John 5:14-15).

In conclusion, if you are in a relationship that is impure, then you are part of relationship that is not from God. "...The body is not meant for sexual immorality, but for the Lord, and the Lord for the body. By his power God raised the Lord from the dead, and he will raise us also. Do you not know that your bodies are members of Christ himself? Shall I then take the members of Christ and unite them with a prostitute? Never! Do you not know that he who united himself with a prostitute is one with her own body? For it is said, 'The two will become one flesh.' But he who unites himself with the Lord is one with him in spirit" (1 Corinthians 6"13-17).

Chapter 7

ENCOURAGEMENT AND SUPPORT

----

*"Do not let any unwholesome talk come
out of your mouths, but only what is
helpful for building others up according
to their needs, that it may benefit those
who listen".*

Ephesians 4:29

What if he never told you that you were special, or failed to mention how wonderful he thinks you are and never shared that he is happy to have you in his life? Uhm,...well men need encouragement too. Not only do they need it, it is vital to their ability to attain their goals. He is in the business of winning the game and you are the cheerleader yelling for him on the sideline. You can be an enthusiastic supporter and boost his morale while he is losing the game, cheer him on when he is winning or give up now. The remainder of this chapter is for the cheerleaders confident that their future mate is a winner--- of not only this game but many more to come.

Though not often discussed, men need reassurance just as women do. They are unlikely to ask for it, but will not shrink from it either. Possibly the only indication you will ever receive to show you he appreciates your reassurance is the few times he will say thanks. But by no means did your simple but kind remark go unnoticed. Men express their appreciation differently from women. Be assured that he recognizes your extra effort.

Men wait all their lives on a woman who will support and encourage them. Why? Because it makes him feel like a man. Therefore, every opportunity you have to share words of encouragement with him is an opportunity to make him pleased with you. Take advantage of this. Constant reassurance is the key. Have you ever been complimented too much by the one you love? Each time you are in his presence or speaking by phone is another opportunity to encourage him. Do not concern yourself about boosting his ego too much because that is impossible. *Help me Lord to speak into his Life ahead*

How can supporting him make him feel like a man? Men strive to fulfill an obligation first to God, themselves and lastly to their mate. These obligations bring pressure on him because he is always wondering if he is doing a good job. If you are reassuring him, then this supports his belief that he can be the man of God that he is called to be. On the contrary, when you bring attention to his blunders you are damaging his self-esteem. It is important to lift him up and to never—I repeat never tear him down. If you make the mistake and do this too often, your relationship will take a turn for the worse. *Help me hard to abide by you, that I may walk w/ no doubt you are present and*

There are things you can do to ensure you are always uplifting. 1) Think before you speak, 2) emphasize the positive versus the negative and 3) respond to him the way you would like for him to respond to you.

Think before you speak

For many of you, this will be difficult. As humans we tend to respond immediately. Our natural reflex is to speak without thinking. A wise woman knows to choose her words carefully because she knows the damage that can be done if she does not. Before voicing an opinion, think of what it is that you are trying to communicate. This will assist you in making a decision about your choice of words. Capture your thoughts and you will be better prepared to choose your words carefully. You will learn to relay messages in a positive rather than negative manner if you do this constantly.

People, especially men, respond better to positive speech. A man will not be responsive to demands and ultimatums. "A gentle answer turns away wrath, but a harsh word stirs up anger" (Proverbs 15:1). Men are natural rebels and put up defenses when placed in uncompromising situations. You will have better luck selling sno cones in Alaska than you will communicating with a man after you have backed him into a corner. *Help me to think before speaking to the man of God, take negative thoughts from me, let*

Positive versus negative *my words be uplifting to the man of God, that he may be at peace at all times in my presence. Amen*

"Do not let any unwholesome talk come out of your mouths, but only what is helpful for building others up according to their needs, that it may benefit others who listen" (Ephesians 4:29). Before saying anything think positively about the situation. There is good in everything if you take the time to find it. "Love must be sincere. Hate what is evil; cling to what is good" (Romans 12:9). God's word teaches us that love must be sincere. When you love someone you focus on the good and desire what is best for them. As sinners we all make mistakes but we do not need others focusing on our mistakes. Instead we need others to lift us up.

A man must feel that you support him. Encouraging words are one way to demonstrate your support. Never should you say things that do not build him up or do things that do not support him. There is a kind way to say and do everything. Therefore because of your love for him let only kind things come from your lips. This is how you show him you love him. *Let the Law of kindness depart from my Lips at all times. I need your help Lord please guide me amen*

Responding in love

Responding in love is to act and say only those things that Jesus would say. It reminds me of the slogan, 'What Would Jesus Do?' (WWJD) In every encounter with your mate or potential mate ask yourself, "What would Jesus do?" If this is your thought prior to everything you say and do, then you will become a loving, patient, kind woman of God who will respond like Jesus.

In addition, before responding, think of how you would like for others to respond to you. Show kindness and let love flow from your lips through the words you choose. "Be kind and compassionate to one another, forgiving each other, just as in Christ God forgave you" (Ephesians 4:32). This is God's instruction for all his children. *"My command is this: Love each other as I have loved you"* (John 15:12). *Help and make me to love agape those around me amen*

There are several things you can do to prove to him that you truly love and respect him. If you truly believe in him then he will know it. Your actions show him how you feel. It is important to determine if you truly believe in your mate. How do you do this? By determining the answer to two simple questions.

- Do you trust his judgment? — *Lord I submit*
- Do you follow his lead? — *to the man of God's judgment and his lead from this day forward, help me to be conscious of what I just prayed amen.*

81

When you trust someone you have confidence in their abilities and firmly rely on them. Whether it is pertaining to a job, purchasing a home or leading you into a closer relationship with God you trust their ability to accomplish the task. You have faith in the unseen and hope for a better tomorrow. Basically, you are totally committed to the desires of your mate and dedicated to your commitment of being his helpmate.

On the contrary, if you do not trust his judgment then you are inclined not to follow his lead. You will not follow someone or something that you are uncertain about. As the helpmate you are to trust your mate's judgment because he is the head. You will never learn to be submissive or to follow his lead if you cannot trust his judgment.

Women are very independent due in part to today's society encouraging women to head households. The Bible specifically states that women are to assist their mates. A helpmate helps and a head of household leads. "...I will make a helper suitable for him" (Genesis 2:18). Regardless of how much money you make or education you receive, your role is to serve as a helper. Therefore, you will never be complete attempting to fulfill the role society has enforced upon you. Trust God and allow him to lead your mate as your mate leads you. Have faith in God first and through obedience, prayer and perseverence you will receive the many blessings God has in store for you. You will then begin to believe in your mate.

Once you begin to trust his judgment and follow his lead, you will learn to have confidence in him. Your mate depends on

to put these into practice now I vow
as I walk w/ the 82 man of God from
this day forward. I pray signs, and wonders
shall follow amen!
Help me O

you and oftentimes 'you only.' He needs you to build him up. Though he may not verbalize this, everything he does is for you. You must show him how much you appreciate him. There are many little things he does that you should be thankful for and these things are not too small for you to notice.

There are various ways to encourage him. Tell him how handsome he is or how great he looks in a particular shirt. Encourage him to have an awesome day and give him a call just to ensure that his day is going well. Express to him how much you like the sweater he wears and how proud you were of him when he handled a situation. Thank him for explaining to you how the video recorder works or how appreciative you were that he called to wake you up. When your focus is on building him up you will have very little time to remember the little mistakes he makes. With consistent encouragement you will be able to sit back, relax and watch your man transform into a confident, loving man who will be quick to reciprocate.

Lastly, believe in him with all your heart. God blessed you with an awesome man of God and you are relying on your judgment to determine what he is capable of doing. Just as you were brought into the light from darkness so was your mate. God equips us all with the things we need. He blesses us according to our conduct and never allows a righteous man to go hungry. With this understanding, you must examine your heart and determine who's ability you are questioning—man's or God's.

Your mate needs for you to believe in him regardless of how

many times he makes mistakes. God allows you to make mistakes everyday. You must forgive, forget and move on. What if God kept record of your wrongs and judged you according to them? Do not make the mistake of becoming self-righteous focusing on what your mate does incorrectly. Direct your attention to what he is doing right.

As the helpmate you are to follow his lead and trust his judgment having complete confidence that he is being led by God. If you believe that he is being led by God, then you will begin to believe in him wholeheartedly. Ultimately, you will respond differently because you know that regardless of what happens, God is still in control.

Chapter **8**

SUSTAIN AND BUILD THE RELATIONSHIP

---

*"If you have any encouragement
from being united with Christ, if
any comfort from is love, if any
fellowship with the Spirit, if any
tenderness and compassion, then
make my joy complete by being like-
minded, having the same love, being one
in spirit and purpose."*

Philippians 2:1-2

You are now prepared for the most loving and rewarding relationship you have ever experienced. You have discovered new ways to relate to others and are now prepared to be in relationships that will fulfill your desires. Using God's word as your standard will provide you with true meaningful relationships with others. God will bless your relationships because you have chosen to do things His way and not your way. As the helpmate, you understand your role and now your mate can fulfill his role as the head. Your life has just taken a turn for the better and your relationships will take on a whole new meaning .

But you are not fully equipped without understanding what it will take to build and sustain this wonderful relationship. Love is a beautiful thing, but it does take work. You must be totally committed to making this union work no matter what challenges you face. This is the importance of having God in the midst of your relationship. It is unwise to be committed to a relationship that is not blessed by God.

Commitment is to pledge oneself to a position. The position you must pledge yourself to is to remain a part of the relationship forever. This type of pledge will not allow you to consider any other option as a means to separate yourself from the relationship. Jesus wants us to be as totally committed to others as he is to us. What if Jesus separated himself from us because of our sin? "As the father has loved me, so have I loved you. Now remain in my love, just as I have obeyed my Father's command and remain in his love" (John 15:9-10). When you are committed to something you will do everything in your power to endure. Honest and open communication will allow the relation to grow and help you remain focused on the commitment you both share. It is important to be open with your mate and express all feelings. Do not hesitate to communicate feelings of discontentment, hurt or disappointment. Your mate can not assist you or make changes within himself if he does not know that you have concerns.

Before discussing a situation, pray about it. Ask God to help you see your heart. It is wise to know your motives for expressing concern, therefore ask yourself if you are being selfish or inconsiderate. Decide if the issue is worth discussing. If it is, then ask God to place in your heart the words you need to say. When expressing concern, do so in a loving manner. Men are not perfect and do not profess to be. Allow him to make mistakes and be a helpmate by helping him correct those mistakes. When you go to him, have a plan to help him see how he can assist you in solving the problem. Give him suggestions on ways to improve, but do not be disappointed if he does not immediately take your advice.

Do not rehash a problem or revisit an issue until you have given him an opportunity to correct the problem. Be patient because this may take some time and several conversations before he is able to see his error. Try to address your concerns differently so that he will not be on the defense. Men are not comfortable with repeated dialogue. They consider it nagging, and men do like to be nagged. Pray to God for assistance in helping you translate your feelings in a manner that will not disturb your mate.

Also before speaking with your mate a second time, consult God about your specific concerns. In addition, sharing a scripture with your mate will allow God's word to correct him and will help you better convey your point. As a man of God most

87

often he will respond after listening to you, but will be more urgent about changing if you use God's word to encourage him. Do not allow Satan to jeopardize your happiness by allowing him to use minor situations to cause you to be ungodly with your mate.

Satan does not want you to be happy. He finds joy in your suffering and wants nothing more than to make you miserable. Specifically through relationships with others is how Satan will cause you to be unrighteous. He will use the most minute occurrence to threaten the stability of your relationship. "Be self-controlled and alert. Your enemy the devil prowls around like a roaring lion looking for someone to devour" (1 Peter 5:8). Do not be deceived thinking that he will not tempt you where your relationship is concerned. Just as Satan tempted Jesus, he will also tempt you.

[handwritten note: Lord Teach me to be patient with the man of God, Help me to not be selfish in my motives will communicat Help me to see the hand of the enemy in our Relationship amen!]

Satan tempts Jesus

" 'Jesus, full of the Holy Spirit, returned from the Jordan and was led by the Spirit in the desert, where for forty days he was tempted by the devil. He ate nothing during those days, and at the end of them was hungry.

The devil said to him, "If you are the Son of God, tell this stone to become bread."
Jesus answered, "It is written: 'Man does not live by bread alone.'

The devil led him up to a high place and showed him in an instant all the kingdoms of the world. And he said to him, "I will give you all their authority and splendor, for it has been given to me, and I can give it to any one I want to. So if you worship me, it will all be yours."

Jesus answered, "It is written: 'Worship the Lord your God and serve him only."

The devil led him to Jerusalem and had him stand on the highest point of his temple. "If you are the Son of God," he said, "throw yourself down from here. For it is written:

"He will command his angels
concerning you to guard you carefully;
they will lift you up in their hands,
so that you will not strike your foot
against a stone.'
Jesus answered, "It says: 'Do not put the Lord your God to the test.'

When the devil had finished all his tempting, he left him until an opportune time. ' " (Luke 4:1-13).

Since Satan's goal is to seek you out and destroy you, you must be on guard. Do not allow him to use your relationship as a means to bring you unhappiness. Stay in prayer with your mate in order to protect yourselves from his schemes. "Do not be afraid of those who kill the body but cannot kill the soul. Rather, be afraid of the One who can destroy both soul and body in hell" (Matthew 10:28). Be wise and use the difficulties you experience in the relationship as opportunities to grow closer to your mate, not as opportunities for Satan to get a foothold and destroy the love you have for each other.

Forgiveness is how God expects his children to remain in his love. Be urgent about forgiving you mate. "Forgive as the Lord forgave you" (Colossians 3:13). "...for all have sinned and fall short of the Glory of God and are justified freely by his grace through the redemption that came by Christ Jesus" (Romans 3:23-24). Remember just as your mate makes mistakes so will you. With each negative experience, learn a new way to improve your own character. "Be kind and compassionate to one another, forgiving each other, just as in Christ God forgave you" (Ephesians 4:32).

Love is what proves to others that you are of Christ. It will take love for you to forgive because it is not always easy to forgive once you have been hurt by the one you love. Feelings of betrayal and anguish will leave you with entangled emotions. It is naive to think that because you are spiritual and have learned God-like ways that forgiving will be easy. But, just as you are open to express love, you must also be able to express forgiveness. "Bear with each other and forgive whatever grievances you may have against one another" (Colossians 3:13).

You must be urgent about going to your mate and expressing your feelings to him. "If you forgive anyone, I also forgive him. And what I have forgiven —if there was anything to forgive—I have forgiven in the sight of Christ for your sake, in order that Satan might not outwit us. For we are not unaware of his schemes" (2 Corinthians 2:10-11). If you are unwilling to be honest with your mate about how you feel, then you will be unable to forgive him. Consequently, the devil will use these types of situations against you. Eventually, your thoughts will lead you into sin and you will begin to emotionally distance yourself from your mate.

Whenever there is conflict, you must take the initiative to make things better. Men have egos which sometimes get in the way of their ability to be humble. As the helpmate, assist him in communicating his feelings. If you approach him with love and humility, he will listen to you. The sooner you discuss situations with him the better. No situation should be left unaddressed. There must be an urgency about resolving matters. I call it the M&M method.

The rule is the 'minute' a situation arises is the 'moment' it must be discussed. To wait even an hour is too long. Evening is too late to discuss an issue that occurred early in the day. If he has a concern, it is to your benefit to be urgent about helping him sort out his feelings. Love your mate enough to want to always see him happy. "Above all, love each other deeply, because love covers a multitude of sins. Offer hospitality to one another without grumbling" (1 Peter 4:8-9). If you are both urgent about resolving conflict, then there will more time for love and less time for conflict. Love never fails" (1 Corinthians 13:8).

Of course, in times of anger for lack of a better word, it is wise to pray about your feelings of bitterness. You must respect each other at all times never displaying anger while communicating. Be slow to speak in times of discontentment. Again, think about what it is that you are attempting to express to your mate. "It is not rude, it is not self-seeking, it is not easily angered, it keeps no record of wrongs. Love does not delight in evil, but rejoices with the truth" (1 Corinthians 13:6).

Lastly R-E-S-P-E-C-T your mate. The Bible states that you are to place others above yourself. "...Honor one another above yourselves" (Romans 12:10). To honor is to respect with complete admiration. Respecting each other is mandatory to making the relationship last and determines the longevity of happiness you have in the relationship. Without respect, the love you have for each other will always be put to the test, and regardless of how long the relationship may last, it will never provide either of you with the happiness you truly deserve.

Respect means humbling out, being patient with each other and forgiving when it seems impossible to forgive. When interacting with your mate, respect him in the utmost way. Put his needs before your own because this is love. Placing your mate's needs before your own means that you treat him better than you would yourself. When both of you are doing this, the relationship will inevitably be a success. "He who pursues righteousness and love finds life, prosperity and honor" (Proverbs 21:21). God blesses obedience, and he will make your path easy when you strive to do his will.

Reevaluate your purpose, which is to love, and realize that

there are no limits when it comes to what God can and will do for you. Grasp the reality that if you are committed to doing God's will and being about his business, he will handle the rest of your business. Good luck with your relationships. Remember above all — "...God is love..." (1 John 4:16)---and as long as you have God, you have all the love you will ever truly need.

Lord I desire to obey your word. and to live by the word of God. Help me Lord prepare me for times to come, Help me to be patient in my love. for the man of God, Help to respect him and help me to not be selfish in putting him before myself. I want to be a virtous woman. the proverbs 31 woman honest. I want to be gentle and meek, I desire to be humble honest and submissive to the man of God. who is after your own heart. teach me how to walk in these things I rebuke the hand of the enemy in this God ordained relationship. Lord I pray that you will take controll of this mind and guide me because I need you and can not do it with out you. I pray for discernment that I may know good from evil. I also pray for wisdom, knowledge and understanding amen.

93

WAYS TO SUSTAIN YOUR RELATIONSHIP

1. Be a spiritual woman at all times.

2. Pray that God will always be in the midst of your relationship.

3. Read the Bible together daily.

4. Always be honest.

5. Allow him to be the head.

6. Always communicate.

7. Be gentle.

8. Listen to him.

9. Be submissive to your mate.

10. Do not nag.

WAYS TO BUILD YOUR RELATIONSHIP

1. Pray about your relationship daily.

2. Be a loving, supportive mate.

3. Create new ways to say you love him.

4. Make his life easier.

5. Always make time for him.

6. Share your true feelings with him.

7. Express your love for him daily.

8. Deny yourself sometimes.

9. Build him up, never tear him down.

10. Correct with kindness.

Chapter **9**

SCRIPTURES TO HELP YOU GROW

-----------------------------   ----------------------------

The following scriptures are for your growth as a woman striving to live for God. Read them daily and make every effort to learn them. Share them with others as you speak so that they will become placed in your heart forever.

MEMORY VERSES

1. No one from the east or west or from the desert can exalt a man. But it is God who judges: He brings one down, he exalts another.

Psalm 75:6-7

---

2. Those who hope in the Lord will renew their strength. They will soar like wings on eagles; they will run and not grow weary, they will walk and not be faint. The Lord will fight for you; you need only to be still.

Isaiah 40:31

---

3. "Do not let this Book of the Law depart from your mouth; meditate on it day and night, so that you will be careful to do everything written in it. Then you will be prosperous and successful."

Joshua 1:8

---

4. But if serving the Lord seems undesirable to you, then choose for yourselves this day whom you will serve, whether the Gods your forefathers served beyond the River, or the Gods of the Amorites, in whose land you are living. But as for me and my household, we will serve the Lord.

Joshua 24:15

5. "Blessed is the man who trusts in the Lord, whose confidence is in him. He will be like a tree planted by the water that sends out its roots by the stream. It does not fear when heat comes; its leaves are always green. It has no worries in a year of drought and never fails to bear fruit."

Jeremiah 17:7-8

6. For the eyes of the Lord range throughout the earth to strengthen those who hearts are fully committed to him.

2 Chronicles 16:9

7. Submit to God and be at peace with him; in this way prosperity will come to you. Accept instruction from his mouth and lay up his words in your heart.

Job 22:21-22

8. And he said to man, "The fear of the Lord—that is wisdom, and to shun evil is understanding."

Job 28:28

9.   Blessed is the man who does not walk in the counsel of the wicked or stand in the way of sinners or sit in the seat of mockers.

Psalm 1:1

---

10.   The words of the Lord are flawless, like silver refined in a furnace of clay, purified seven times.

Psalm 12:6

---

11.   The Law of the Lord is perfect, reviving the soul. The statutes of the Lord are trustworthy, making wise the simple. The precepts of the Lord are right , giving joy to the heart. The commands of the Lord are radiant, giving light to the eyes. The fear of the Lord is pure, enduring forever. The ordinances of the Lord are sure and altogether righteous. They are more precious than gold, than much pure gold; they are sweeter than honey from the comb. By them is your servant warned; in keeping them there is a great reward.

Psalm 19:7-11

---

12.   May the words of my mouth and the meditation of my heart be pleasing in your sight, O Lord, my Rock and my Redeemer.

Psalm 19:14

---

13. The earth is the Lord's, and everything in it, the world, and all who live in it.

Psalm 24:1

---

14. The Lord is my light and my salvation—whom shall I fear? The Lord is the stronghold of all my life—of whom shall I be afraid?

Psalm 27:1

---

15. His anger lasts only a moment, but his favor lasts a lifetime; weeping may remain for a night, but rejoicing comes in the morning.

Psalm 30:5

---

16. A righteous man may have many troubles, but the Lord delivers him from them all.

Psalm 34:19

---

17. Delight yourself in the Lord and he will give you the desires of your heart.

Psalm 37:4

---

18.   "Be still, and know that I am God; I will be exalted among the nations, I will be exalted in the earth."

Psalm 46:10

---

19.   Create in me a pure heart, O God, and renew a steadfast spirit within me. Restore to me a joy of your salvation and grant me a willing spirit, to sustain me.

Psalm 51: 10-12

---

20.   Evening, morning and noon I cry out in distress, and he hears my voice.

Psalm 55:17

---

21.   For the Lord God is a sun and shield; the Lord bestows favor and honor; no good thing does he withhold from those whose walk is blameless.

Psalm 84:11

---

22.   How can a young man keep his way pure? By living according to your word.

Psalm 119:9

23. To all perfection I see a limit; but your commands are boundless. Oh, how I love your law! I meditate on it all day long. Your commands make me wiser than my enemies, for they are ever with me. I have more insight than all my teachers, for I meditate on your statutes. I have more understanding than the elders, for I obey your precepts.

Psalm 119:96-100

24. Your word is a lamp to my feet and a light for my path.

Psalm 119:105

25. Trust in the Lord with all your heart lean not on your own understanding; in all your ways acknowledge him, and he will make your paths straight.

Proverbs 3:5-6

26. There is a way that seems right to a man, but in the end it leads to death.

Proverbs 14:12

27.   There is a time for everything, and a season for every
        activity under heaven.

Ecclesiastes 3:1

28.   "Come now, let us reason together," says the Lord.
        "Though your sins are like scarlet, they shall be as white as
        snow; though they are red as crimson, they shall be like
        wool."

Isaiah 1:18

29.   Whether you turn to the right or to the left, your ears will
        hear a voice behind you saying, "This is the way; walk in it."

Isaiah 30:21

30.   The grass withers and the flowers fall, but the word of the
        God stands forever.

Isaiah 40:8

31.   Your iniquities have separated you from God; your sins have
        hidden his face from you, so that you will not hear.

Isaiah 59:2

32.   "Before they call I will answer; while they are still speaking
        I will hear."

Isaiah 65:24

---

33.   "For I know the plans I have for you, declares the Lord,
        plans to prosper you and not to harm you, plans to give you
        hope and a future. Then you will call on me and come and
        pray to me, and I will listen to you. You will seek me
        with all your heart."

Jeremiah 29:11-13

---

34.   "I am the Lord, the God of all mankind. Is anything too
        hard for me?"

Jeremiah   32:27

---

35.   The Lord is good, a refuge in times of trouble. He cares for
        those who trust in him.

Nahum 1:7

---

36.   "For if you forgive men when they sin against you, your

heavenly Father will also forgive you."

---

37.   "So do not worry, saying, What shall we eat? or What shall
       we drink? or What shall we wear? For the pagans run after
       all these things, and your heavenly Father knows that you
       need them.   But seek first his Kingdom and his
       righteousness, and all these things will be given to you as
       well."

Matthew 6:31-33

---

38.   "Ask and it will be given to you; knock and the door will be
       opened to you. For everyone who asks receives; he who
       seeks finds; and to him who knocks, the door will be
       opened."

Matthew 7:7-8

---

39.   "Enter through the narrow gate. For wide is the gate and
       broad is the road that leads to destruction, and many enter
       through it. But small is the gate and narrow the road that
       leads to life, and only a few find it."

Matthew 7:13-14

---

40. "Not everyone who says to me, "Lord, Lord," will enter the Kingdom of heaven, but only he who does the will of my Father who is in heaven."

Matthew 7:21

---

41. "Whoever acknowledges me before men, I will also acknowledge him before my Father in heaven. But whoever disowns me before men, I will disown him before my Father in heaven."

Matthew 10:33-33

---

42. "Come to me, all you who are weary and burdened, and I will give you rest."

Matthew 11:28

---

43. "Then Jesus said to his disciples, 'If anyone would come after me, he must deny himself and take up his cross and follow me. For whoever wants to save his life will lose it, but whoever loses his life for me will find it.' "

Matthew 16:24-25

---

44. "Again, I tell you that if two of you on earth agree about anything you ask for, it will be done for you by my Father in

heaven. For where two or three come together in my name, there am I with them."

Matthew 18:19-20

---

45.   "If you believe, you will receive whatever you ask for in prayer."

Matthew 21:22

---

46.   "Have faith in God," Jesus answered. "I tell you the truth, if anyone says to this mountain, 'Go throw yourself into the sea,' and does not doubt in his heart but believes that what he says will happen, it will be done for him."

Mark 11:22-23

---

47.   "Therefore I tell you, whatever you ask for in prayer, believe that you have received it, and it will be yours."

Mark 11:24

---

48.   "Do not let your hearts be troubled. Trusts in God; trust also in me. In my Father's house are many rooms, if it were not so, I would have told you.   I am going to prepare a place for you, I will come back and take you to be with me

that you also may be where I am."

John 14:1-3

---

49.   "Peace I leave with you; my peace I give you. I do not give
to you as the world gives. Do not let your hearts be
troubled and do not be afraid."

John 14:27

---

50.   "I am the vine; you are the branches. If a man remains in
me and I in him, he will bear much fruit; apart from me you
can do nothing. If anyone does not remain in me, he is like
a branch that is thrown away and withers; such branches are
picked up, thrown into the fire and burned. If you remain in
me and my words remain in you, ask whatever you wish,
and it will be given to you. This is to my Father's glory, that
you bear much fruit, showing yourselves to be my disciples."

John 15:5-8

---

51.   We also rejoice in our sufferings, because we know that
sufferings produces perseverance; perseverance, character;
and character, hope.

Romans 5:3-4

111

52.   For the wages of sin is death, but the gift of God is eternal life in Christ Jesus our Lord.

Romans 6:23

---

53.   Now if we are children, then we are heirs of God and coheirs with Christ, if indeed we share in his sufferings in order that we may also share in his glory. I consider that out present sufferings are not worth comparing with the glory that will be revealed in us.

Romans 8:17-18

---

54.   And we know that in all things God works for the good of those who love him, who have been called according to his purpose.

Romans 8:28

---

55.   What, then, shall we say in response to this? If God is for us, who can be against us?

Romans 8:31

---

56.   No, in all these things we are more than conquerors through him who loved us. For I am convinced that neither life nor

death, neither angels nor demons, neither the present nor the future, nor any powers, neither height nor depth, nor anything else in all creation, will be able to separate us from the love of God that is in Christ Jesus our Lord.

Romans 8:37-39

---

57.   Therefore, I urge you, brothers, in view of God's mercy, to offer your bodies as living sacrifices, holy and pleasing to God----this is your spiritual act of worship. Do not conform any longer to the pattern of this world, but be transformed by the renewing of your mind...

Romans 12:1-2

---

58.   For the message of the cross is foolishness to those who are perishing, but to us who are being saved it is the power of God.

1 Corinthians 1:25

---

59.   However, as it is written: "No eye has seen, no ear has heard, no mind has conceived what God has prepared for those who love him.

1 Corinthians 2:9

---

60. Don't you know that you yourselves are God's temple and that God's Spirit lives in you?

1 Corinthians 3:16

---

61. Do you not know that the wicked will not inherit the kingdom of God? Do not be deceived: Neither the sexually immoral nor idolaters nor adulterers nor male prostitutes nor homosexual offenders nor thieves nor the greedy nor the drunkards nor slanderers nor swindlers will inherit the kingdom of God.

1 Corinthians 6:9-10

---

62. No temptation has seized you except what is common to man. And God is faithful; he will not let you be tempted beyond what you can bear. But when you are tempted, he will also provide a way out so that you can stand up under it.

1 Corinthians 10:13

---

63. Love is patient, love is kind. It does not envy, it does not boast, it is not proud. It is not rude, it is not self-seeking, it is not easily angered, it keeps no record of wrongs. Love does not delight in evil but rejoices with the truth. It always protects, always trusts, always hopes, always perseveres.

64.   Now it is God who makes both us and you stand firm in
        Christ. He anointed us, set his seal of ownership on us, and
        put his Spirit in our hearts as a deposit, guaranteeing what
        is to come.

2 Corinthians 1:21-22

65.   For our light and momentary troubles are achieving for us an
        eternal glory that far outweighs them all.

2 Corinthians 4:8-9

66.   So we fix our eyes not on what is seen, but on what is
        unseen. For what is seen is temporary, but what is unseen
        is eternal.

2 Corinthians 4:18

67.   For we must all appear before the judgment seat of Christ,
        that each one may receive what is due him for the things
        done while in the body, whether good or bad.

2 Corinthians 5:10

68. Do not be yoked together with unbelievers. For what do righteousness and wicked have in common? Or what fellowship can light have with darkness? What harmony is there between Christ and Belial? What does a believer have in common with an unbeliever? What agreement is there between the temple of God and idols? As God has said: "I will live with them and walk among them, and I will be their God, and they will be my people."

2 Corinthians 6:14-16

69. To keep me from being conceited because of these surpassingly great revelations, there was given me a thorn in my flesh, a messenger of Satan, to torment me. Three times I pleaded with the Lord to take it away from me. But he said to me, "My grace is sufficient for you, for my power is made perfect in weakness." Therefore I will boast all the more gladly about my weaknesses, so that Christ's power may rest on me. That is why for Christ's sake, I delight in weaknesses, in insults, in hardships, in persecutions, in difficulties. For when I am weak, then I am strong.

2 Corinthians 12:7-10

70. So I say, live by the Spirit, and you will not gratify the desires of the sinful nature. For the sinful nature desires what is contrary to the Spirit, and the Spirit contrary to the sinful nature. They are in conflict with each other, so that

you do not do what you want.

---

71. But the fruit of the Spirit is love, joy, peace, patience, kindness, goodness, faithfulness, gentleness and self-control. Against such things there is no law.

Galatians 5: 22-23

---

72. Do not be deceived: God cannot be mocked. A man reaps what he sows. The one who sows to please his sinful nature, from that nature will reap destruction; the one who sows to please the Spirit, from the Spirit will reap eternal life. Let us not become weary in doing good, for at the proper time we will reap a harvest if we do not give up.

Galatians 6:7-9

---

73. In your anger do not sin: Do not let the sun go down while you are angry, and do not give the devil a foothold.

Ephesians 4:26-27

---

74. Wives, submit to your husbands as to the Lord.

Ephesians 5:22

117

75. Do not be anxious about anything, but in everything, by prayer and petition, with thanksgiving, present your requests to God. And the peace of God, which transcends all understanding, will guard your hearts and your minds in Christ Jesus.

Philippians 4:6-7

76. I can do everything through him who gives me strength.

Philippians 4:11-13

77. Be joyful always; pray continually; give thanks in all circumstances, for this is God's will for you in Christ Jesus.

1 Thessalonians 4:16-17

78. For God did not give us a spirit of timidity, but a spirit of power, of love and of self-discipline.

2 Timothy 1:7

79. Do your best to present yourself to God as one approved, a workman who does not need to be ashamed and who correctly handles the word of truth.

2 Timothy 2:15

80.	Nevertheless, God's solid foundation stands firm, sealed with this inscription: "The Lord knows those who are his," and "Everyone who confesses the name of the Lord must turn away from wickedness."

2 Timothy 2:19

81.	Now faith is being sure of what we hope for and certain of what we do not see.

Hebrews 11:1

82.	And without faith it is impossible to please God, because anyone who comes to him must believe that he exists and that he rewards those who earnestly seek him.

Hebrews 11:6

83.	So we say with confidence, "The Lord is my helper; I will not be afraid. What can man do to me?"

Hebrews 13:6

84.	Consider it pure joy, my brothers, whenever you face trials of many kinds, because you know that the testing of your faith develops perseverance. Perseverance must finish its work so that you may be mature and complete, not lacking anything.

James 1: 2-4

---

85.   My dear brothers, take note of this: Everyone should be quick to listen, slow to speak and slow to become angry, for man's anger does not bring about the righteous life that God desires.

James 1:19-20

---

85.   Submit yourselves, then, to God. Resist the devil, and he will flee from you. Come near to God and he will come near to you.

James 4: 7-8

---

86.   ...The prayer of a righteous man is powerful and effective.

James 5:16

---

87.   Wives, in the same way be submissive to your husbands so that, if any of them do not believe the word, they may be won over without words by the behavior of their wives,

when they see the purity and reverence of your lives.

1 Peter 3:1-2

---

88. Cast all your anxiety on him because he cares for you. Be self-controlled and alert. Your enemy the devil prowls around like a roaring lion looking for someone to devour.

1 Peter 5:7-8

---

89. Do not love the world or anything in the world. If anyone loves the world, the love of the Father is not in him. For everything in the world—the cravings of the sinful man, the lust in his eyes and the boasting of what he has and does—comes not from the Father but from the world.

1 John 2:15-16

---

90. No one who is born of God will continue to sin, because God's seed remains in him; he cannot go on sinning, because he has been born of God.

1 John 3:9

---

91. This is the confidence we have in approaching God: that if

we ask anything according to his will, he hears us—whatever we ask—we know that we have what we asked of him.

92.   Many are plans in a man's heart, but it is the Lord's purpose that prevails.

Proverbs 19:21

93.   The acts of the sinful nature are obvious: sexual immorality, impurity, debauchery; idolatry and witchcraft; hatred, discord, jealousy, fits of rage, selfish ambition, dissensions, factions and envy, drunkenness, orgies and the like. I warn you as I did before, that those who live like this will not inherit the kingdom of God.

Galatians 5:19-21

94.   But among you there must not be even a hint of sexual immorality, or of any kind of impurity, or of greed, because these are improper for God's holy people.

Ephesians 5:3

95. Trust in the Lord with all your heart and lean not on your own understanding; in all your ways acknowledge him and he will make your paths straight.

Proverbs 3:5-6

---

96. "...Always be prepared to give an answer to everyone who asks you to give the reason for the hope that you have.

1 Peter 3:15

---

97. He replied, "Because you have so little faith. I tell you the truth, if you have faith as small as a mustard seed, you can go say to this mountain, 'Move from here to there' and it will move. Nothing will be impossible for you.

Matthew 17:20-21

---

98. No one born of God will continue to sin, because God's seed remains in him; he cannot go on sinning because he has been born of God.

1 John 3:9

---

99. Therefore do not worry about tomorrow, for tomorrow will worry about itself. Each day has enough trouble of its own.

Matthew 6:34

100.   "A wife of a noble character who can find?
        She is worth far more than rubies.
        Her husband has full confidence in her
        and lacks nothing of value.
        She brings him good, not harm all the days of her life.
        She selects wool and flax
        and works with eager hands.
        She is like the merchant ships, bringing her food from afar.
        She gets up while it is still dark;
        She provides food for her family
        and portions for her servant girls.
        She considers a field and buys it;
        out of her earnings she plants a vineyard.
        She sets about her work vigorously;
        her arms are strong for her tasks.
        She sees that her trading is profitable,
        and her lamp does not go out at night.
        In her hand she holds the distaff
        and grasps the spindle with her fingers.
        She opens her arms to the poor
        and extends her hands to the needy.
        When it snows, she has no fear for her household;
        for all of them are clothed in scarlet.
        She makes coverings for her bed;
        she is clothed in fine linen and purple.
        Her husband is respected at the city gate,

where he takes his seat among the elders of the land.
She makes linen garments and sells them,
and supplies the merchants with sashes.
She is clothed with strength and dignity;
she can laugh at the days to come.
She speaks with wisdom, and faithful instruction is on her
  tongue.
She watches over the affairs of her household
and does not eat the bread of idleness.
Her children arise and call her blessed;
her husband also, and he praises her:
Many women do noble things, but you surpass
  them all.
Charm is deceptive, and beauty is fleeting;
but a woman who fears the Lord is to be praised.
Give her the reward she has earned,
and let her works bring her
praise at the city gate.

Proverbs 31:1-31

ABOUT THE AUTHOR

Helena Lafaye Webster, born in Texarkana, Texas, is currently a full-time graduate student completing a Master of Social Work (MSW) degree in Atlanta, Georgia. She completed her undergraduate degree at Clark Atlanta University and her current interests lie in the area of child and family. She enjoys writing and public speaking.

Her deep love for the lost and the underprivileged inspires her to help those in need. As an author and speaker, she desires to impact the lives of individuals through the talents God has given her by being a vessel to help others accept Christ as their Lord and Savior. She is grateful for the opportunity to reach out to others in this way and thankful to God for His guidance.

As a disciple, mother, an established business owner, student, public speaker and author she keeps herself very busy. Most of her time is spent evangelizing, sharing quality time with her son and keeping the business together. Her love for her son and her desire to be the best she can be is what encouraged her to entitle her next book "Balancing Everything" which is due out next fall.

Be assured that this talented writer is on the move and striving to do great things for her Lord and Savior, Jesus Christ, because she understands from where her strength comes. Therefore, as she would say, "I can do all things through Christ who gives me strength."

GOD'S WAY

I decided today that things will be different
I have tread this road far too long.
Through the pains and joy, laughter and tears,
I look back and wonder where my life has gone.

The path of righteousness always very near,
Though the other road seemed easier once again.
I chose every way except your way God,
And I have paid a heavy price for my Sin.

Satan has taken my joy as he has so many times before,
And thrown it in my face to see.
I did not know then, what I know now Lord;
He too, was just using me.

I can turn to no one and I have no where to turn,
My old ways are of no interest to me anymore.
All I want God is a resting place,
I am tired and weary, please open the door.

I am begging you Father to show me your way,
People have spoken to me about you so much.
Please fill this void I have inside of me,
I long to feel the warmth of your loving touch.

I stand before you humbly with tears in my eyes,
Asking for you to guide me starting today.
I surrender my life and all that I am, I give up.
God, I am now ready to do things Your Way.

Helena Webster

APPENDIX

Dressing To Impress

What is acceptable dress? Dressing is a total look and is not just what you put on, but the overall appearance of a well groomed woman. Ask yourself before you leave your house. Am I dressed appropriately? To always be certain that you can answer this question with a yes, use the five point scale below as guide. As a matter of fact, until you have learned to make this determination without assistance, write these points on a note card and tape them to your mirror.

```
CHECKLIST

1. Hair
2. Face and eyes
3. Hands and nails
4. Clothes
5. Accessories
```

1.   *Hair well groomed*

The hair is clean, neat, and in a style. No ponytails, slick downs, and unkept old styles are accepted. (Note: Ladies once your hair do is done, let it go.)

A woman must be distinctively different from a man in all areas, including her hairstyle. Neatness is important and it is great to have a trim, but the concern is for women who cut there hair in styles similar to men. God made woman in man's image, but the body framework, tone of speech, and complete physical appearance is totally different as God planned for it to be.

Hair in the Old Testament was regarded by the Jews as a mark of beauty and sometimes pride. Baldness was despised.

"Therefore the Lord will bring sores
on the heads of the women of Zion;
the Lord will make their scalps bald.
In that day the Lord will snatch away their finery:
the bangles and headbands and crescent necklaces,
the earrings and bracelets and veils,
the headdresses and ankle chains and sashes,
the perfume bottles and charms,
the signet rings and nose rings,
the fine robes and the capes and cloaks,
the purses and mirrors,
and the linen garments and tiaras and shawls.
Instead of fragrance there will be stench;
instead of a sash, a rope;
instead of well-dressed hair, baldness;
instead of fine clothing, sackcloth;
instead of beauty, branding" (Isaiah 3:17-24).

The point is, men like hair. It is understood that you like your hair short and others compliment you on your great cut but again---men like hair.

2.   *Face*

Your face should have a glowing appearance. It should be clean and smooth. This may mean make-up or seeing a dermatologist. Whichever, a glowing face is a pretty face.

Make-up is wonderful, but too much is a turn-off. Not only does it make it difficult to see your natural beauty, but he may be thinking if he hugs you too often, dry cleaning could get expensive. It is used to enhance your natural beauty, it is not a cover up. More, is definitely not better. Use it sparingly, lightly and with caution. A good way to determine if you have on too much is to look at yourself before you put it on and after you have it on. If you are a more beautiful, glamorous, alluring woman than you were without it, you are probably wearing too much.

It is advised that you visit a make-up counter to learn the proper way to apply make-up. Just because you think you are doing a great job applying your make-up does not mean you are. Scheduling an appointment to have a make-up artist assist you in learning proper application will provide you with new techniques and a different look.

A decision not to wear make-up is a good one too, but just because he told you that you are naturally beautiful, does not mean he wants you to look like him. A little lipstick, chap stick, or lip liner is a must. Smooth lips are a feminine quality that men notice. Don't you notice when someone has dry chapped lips or skin?

Eyes

An eyebrow arch gives the face a manicured look. It will bring attention to your eyes and face. You have your choices of plucking, clipping or waxing. You do not need an arch every week or even every two weeks. Once you have one good arch, you will not need another for at least three months.

Be careful because you do not want to loose your natural eyebrow line. Plucking the hair above the eye too often, will eventually lead to loss of hair. Once the follicle is destroyed, the hair will not grow back.

Maintaining the arch can be done by plucking any hair outside the arch once a week and clipping the longer hairs with small hair scissors.

3.   *Hands*

Your hands tell a lot about you. Many men look a woman's hands to try and determine her age while others use the look of the hands to access how well a woman takes care of herself. Though men will not express these things to you until you have established a closer friendship, they notice much more than women credit them with. Actually, when a man is interested in you there is very little that he does not notice about you. Therefore, your hands should be soft and smooth looking at all times.

The type of lotion you choose can make all the difference. Brands such as Nivea and Lubriderm will provide long-lasting results though they are more expensive than other brands, but any lotion with lanolin, and a silicate is a good choice. In addition, Vitamin E is great for your skin's appearance.

At all times, be certain to carry a small container of lotion in your purse to ensure that you maintain smooth looking hands throughout the day.

Nails

Ladies, can we talk? This new fad with nail tips is out of control. It has done two things; created an opportunity to have beautiful nails and an opportunity to have the most unkept looking hands I have ever seen in my

134

life! If it is not possible to squeeze in a trip to the nail salon at least once a week, then I suggest you let the tips go and wear your own. A little polish on your own nails looks more appealing to a man and the rest of the world, than broken, split, and cracked nails on one hand, while two are missing on the other.

Moreover, a visit to the nail salon to get a manicure is a good idea. Manicures keep your hands looking presentable at all times and a professional job is inexpensive. A manicure once a week will ensure that your hands get the attention they need and will encourage you to focus on the look of your hands.

For those of you who do not wear nail tips, you can have pretty hands without the extra expense of going to a nail salon by spending some quality time on your nails yourself. Approximately forty-five minutes on your nails will give you a fresh manicured look A nail file, buffer and polish is all you will need to have pretty nails in minutes. Take time to treat yourself while at the same time, save money.

4.   *Clothes*

Think clean, ironed, and coordinated and you will never go wrong. No DWI's - dress without ironing. Clean clothes make a statement as does ironed ones. It is not important that you pay top dollar for the clothing you wear, but what is important is that you look neat and like a female. A man is pleased when he has a woman who looks well-groomed. Masculinity is very appealing to us just as femininity is attractive to our male counterparts. A man's initial purpose for approaching you, was that your overall appearance was appealing to him. You are opposite from him in your dress, speech and behavior, and that is attractive to him.

For clarification purposes, feminine clothing is not tight clothing. Dressing feminine means looking like Jill and not Jack. Understandably, you are pleased when you have lost a few pounds, trimmed your figure and toned those areas, but it is wise to leave your newfound figure hidden from the public and left to the imagination. Spandex is great…in the gym, not when you are out to dinner. Men enjoy the unknown just as they enjoy knowing when they take you to that fancy dinner party, you will not be wearing a leopard print body suit. Make him feel confident in your ability to be the woman he expects you to be at all times. "I also want women to dress modestly, with decency and propriety, not with braided hair or gold or pearls or expensive clothes, but with good deeds, appropriate for women who profess to worship God" (2 Timothy 2:9). Looking your best will not only make you look good on the outside, but it will make you feel good on the inside.

5. *Accessories*

Accessories give an overall look of completeness and show that you took the extra time to make yourself look presentable. It is unwise to use each piece of jewelry you own every time you dress, but a watch, one bracelet and a pair of earrings is plenty.

There is a difference in the look of a woman who has on a few accessories and one who does not. Accessories make the style of dress more appealing. Imagine not wearing earrings or a watch with a dress suit and then imagine putting them on.   Just as the watch and earrings will make a difference, a small chain around the neck and a single chain bracelet will also.

"Your beauty should not come from outward adornment, such as braided hair and the wearing of gold jewelry and fine clothes" (1 Peter 3:3). God's word states that your beauty should come from within and not from outward adornment. "..but a prudent wife is from the Lord" (Proverbs 19:14). Prudence means moderation, never too much and never too little. Prudent also means wise in handling practical matters and careful in regard to one's own interests. In using accessories, be practical. It is not advised, that you have on more than three pieces at a time, excluding your watch. A pair of earrings, a bracelet and a necklace are appropriate for any outfit.

To further assist you in learning what accessories to use, look at magazines such as *Glamour, Essence,* and *Vogue.* These magazines have great fashion ideas and can help you learn new ways to wear jewelry, scarves, and many other accessories that are sure to enhance your style of dress.

Remember to ask yourself before you walk out the door, "Am I appropriately dressed?" and "Do I look my very best?". The extra time it will take to look your best is well worth the effort.

God is waiting patiently for you. If you are seeking to grow closer to God, study His word and become a disciple of Christ please feel free to call (404) 508-8200 anytime. You are always welcome to worship with us.